Natural Cooking
the FINNISH Way

Natural
Cooking
the FINNISH Way

ULLA KÄKÖNEN

QUADRANGLE NYT
The New York Times Book Company

Library of Congress Catalog Card Number: 73-89271
International Standard Book Number: 0-8129-0444-3

Book design: Charlotte Thorp

The following recipes first appeared in *Mantsikkamöllöstä apposkaaliin* by
Irja Seppänen-Pora (Kustannusosakeyhtiö Otava, Helsinki): Old Karelian
Mushroom-Barley Soup, Old Karelian Pork Pot, Buckwheat Flat Bread, Uncooked
Pasha, and Old Karelian Egg Pie.

The following recipes first appeared in *Cookbook* by Countess Eva Mannerheim-Sparre
(Kustannusosakeyhtiö Otava, Helsinki): Pork and Cabbage Pot, Pork and Small
Turnip Pot, Lamb and Turnip Pot, and Fried Lamb Kidneys.

Contents

Introduction

When I was a child in Finland, my Karelian grandmother lived with us and did all the cooking. I learned by watching her cook, and by listening to her. She worked rapidly and steadily, with a natural rhythm—talking to me all the time she worked, telling me about what she was doing and why. She never used a cookbook; only her hand and heart. She gave me the feeling that the work of the cook is just a continuation of a natural process begun in the soil.

The three summer months are precious to the Finns, and when I was small we spent them in the country. Our village was not a resort, just a few tiny farms, and we were one of two city families there for the long holiday. The basic, simple cooking and baking in the village reflected the traditional Finnish diet. People lived on what they grew, wasting nothing. After the harvest they lived on what they could preserve for the winter.

Baking day brought the women together. Early in the morning, a wood fire was built to heat an enormous iron oven. Because wood was so valuable, the women shared the oven. Rye bread was baked first because it required the most heat; then the yeast bread, *pulla,* and finally—and only rarely—pastries, cookies, or cakes. Rarely, because butter and eggs were too dear to be used often in foods that, although delicious, were not substantially filling. After the breads were baked, the traditional pot dish was put in the oven to cook in the afterheat. Nothing was wasted, not even heat.

The year-round people of our vacation village knew what would happen at the arrival of my father, who had a mania for fishing. Very early each morning he would be the first man at the lake, dropping his nets for the day's catch. Since the local men always were busy with their farming chores and could not often join him, my father distributed his haul to the neighbors and everyone got some fresh fish. My father had a ritual about smoking fish which involved gathering the juniper branches for the open fire and tending the fish as it smoked. The neighbors all knew that when the ritual was completed he would go from door to door with smoked fish for everyone. My father's devotion to fishing allowed me to see yet another way of living from natural resources, wasting nothing.

Bread and cereal products were really the solid foundation of the Finnish diet. Daily bread was more than a nice phrase. The variety and quality of breads in Finland are still astonishing. A basket of two or three kinds of bread (always including a hard bread) is still found on a Finnish table at any meal of the day.

My grandmother knew the value of good bread even if she didn't know of MIT Professor R. S. Harris who made a study of the breads of fourteen countries. He found the Finnish mixed-grain, or yeast, bread to be the most nutritious, surpassing all the enriched breads that were included in the study.

Milk and sourmilk products were the second most important staple in the diet, and involved us in another cycle of food preparation. Butter was still made in a hand churn. Buttermilk was always a popular table drink. I can remember when the first wheel-driven churn arrived. It seemed to us a great modern invention—all you had to do was turn a wheel and the butter would separate from the buttermilk!

In terms of nutrition, the milk and sourmilk products provided a wide variety of protein and vitamins. The sourmilk products are easy on one's system, because the protein is more easily digested than that of sweet milk and it is also beneficial to the balance of internal bacteria.

In the traditional diet, meat was a rarity, usually reserved for festive occasions. When a cow was butchered, the meat was usually sold to buy more immediate necessities than beef. Pork was the most common meat eaten and is the meat with the highest vitamin B content. Fish was often cooked in such a way that the bones softened and could be eaten. It was said to help the brain grow. At least it was certainly an excellent source of minerals, phosphorus, and calcium.

The only deficiency in the Finnish diet was vitamin C in late winter when root vegetables had lost much of this vitamin and fruits were not readily available. In the summer there were plenty of wild berries to pick.

I loved the country cooking and always looked forward to going to the milk house, as we called the farm from which we bought our milk, after dinner. I was allowed to assist in the milking by standing behind the cow and brushing flies away from her with a birch branch. Then I would go into the house and sit in the corner as if to play with the cat, while the table was being set for supper. If a dish I really liked was being served, I would finally allow myself to be coaxed into eating something, although I had already eaten at home. If it was one of my favorites, like pancakes, I'd eat until I was stuffed. In that house I could drink coffee—something my parents never allowed!

After my grandmother died, cooking in our house entered a new phase based on ready-made convenience foods, which my mother loved, being less than devoted to cooking. She would buy ready-made casseroles and such canned foods as Karelian pot, stroganoff, and pea soup. The menu was still Finnish and of high quality, for the Finnish pots and casseroles, in spite of mass production, are well made and most of them improve in taste when reheated.

My own start as a cook began a third phase: the emulation of everything foreign, spicy, and unusual. My ambition was to burn my friends' mouths with hot peppers. I remember groups of gasping guests, gulping down beer, wine, or water, to recover from the hot spiciness of my exotic dishes.

Only after I had been living in New York City for a while, and began to crave old Karelian pot dishes, did I realize that as a child I had lived in a world of marvelous natural foods and cooking of extraordinary quality. When I looked at the pale yellow vegetables that my greengrocer here called tomatoes, I realized the true richness of my past. I remembered wild mushrooms, tiny, sweet new potatoes dug up just before cooking, sun-kissed and almost sinfully tasty tomatoes, and bread fresh from the oven covered with country butter which I had helped to churn. I recalled the festivity of the fresh salmon my father caught once in a while during those summer days, poached with vegetables and herbs, and the delight of an occasional rich pastry.

I hope I can pass along some of my feelings, through these recipes. I have chosen dishes to represent every aspect of Finnish cooking. Most are old recipes for familiar dishes which are a regular part of the family's menus, even today. Some new recipes I acquired from friends. Some very old recipes came from a book of old Karelian cooking, *Mantsikkamöllöstä apposkaaliin* by Irja Seppänen-Pora. Some are from *Cookbook* by Countess Eva Mannerheim-Sparre, who combines country-manor Finnish cooking with Russian, French, and other continental cuisines.

There are many levels of Finnish cuisine, all of them still found today. Many of the very old, provincial dishes are still enjoyed. Western Finland offers casseroles and cereal dishes. *Savo*, the Middle Finland province, is known for the Fish Rooster or *Kalakukko*, and many of the Lapland specialties are considered rare delicacies. Karelian cooks are known for their baking skills and generous hospitality.

Scandinavian influence is, of course, very strong in the Finnish cuisine. The Russian and Estonian cooking, especially, gave inspiration to Karelian cooks. Karelian specialties, in turn, were more widely introduced to Finnish tables after World War II, when many Karelian refugees settled in various parts of the country.

Almost every cook passing on a recipe knows that hers is not only the best, but the *only* one and therefore I have given many versions of the most common dishes. And while I have tried to present the most basic way of cooking each dish, I have been partial to the ways of my own grandmother. To her I owe much of this book.

Ingredients and Substitutes

Barley: The two types of barley, pearled and hulled, as well as barley flour are available in most health food stores.

Buckwheat: Most health food stores carry buckwheat flour, whole buckwheat, and cracked buckwheat which is also known as kasha. Buy a variety that isn't precooked.

Black currant: Some delicatessens and health food stores carry a black currant drink which can be substituted in cooking if fresh currants are not available.

Crayfish: The Canadian and small Florida crayfish are recommended. They are easily available in coastal areas.

Dill: Fresh dill can be found at many greengrocers. Dry dill or dill seed can be substituted.

European cucumber: A long, dark green cucumber with small tender seeds. Regular or pickling cucumbers can be substituted.

Gluten flour: A protein-rich baking flour which is available in well-stocked health food stores.

Lingonberries: Lingonberry preserves are available in many supermarkets and delicatessens. Cranberry preserves or sauce may be substituted.

Potato starch: This starch makes puddings softer and more transparent than cornstarch does. Available in supermarkets, often in kosher sections, and in health food stores.

Raw sugar: Less processed (but washed for U.S. consumption) white sugar. Regular granulated sugar may be substituted or honey, in all but the baking recipes.

Reindeer meat: Not generally available in America. Venison may be substituted.

Rolled oats: Available in health food stores. Don't use the precooked variety.

Root artichoke or Jerusalem artichoke: A knotty root vegetable sold in specialty greengroceries.

Rutabaga: This large yellow root vegetable is sometimes known as the yellow turnip. The small, white turnip may be substituted if necessary.

Rye flour: Available in health food stores.

Rye malt: This may be found in Scandinavian specialty stores.

Sea salt: Preferred to regular salt because of its high mineral content. Coarse sea salt is used for salting and pickling. Available in health food stores.

Smelts: Small lake smelts, available frozen in many supermarkets, are ideal for most recipes because of their uniform size. Fresh smelts are very good as well.

Unbleached white flour: Unbleached white *pastry* flour is suitable for crisp cookies and pastries. Regular unbleached white flour may be substituted. Both are available in health food stores and in some super-markets.

Whey: The liquid left when solids are separated from milk or buttermilk. Can be used in baking and in some soups.

White pepper: Black pepper can be substituted in all recipes except those for white soups and sauces and delicate salads.

Natural Cooking
the FINNISH Way

Chapter 1

CEREAL SOUPS AND PORRIDGES
[VELLIT JA PUUROT]

If you have ever tasted a homemade cereal dish, you know why precooked cereals have a pale taste compared to the real stuff. To prepare homemade cereals, you need more than 2 minutes; actually a homemade cereal requires only 5 minutes of your time—the remaining 20 to 30 minutes of cooking will take care of itself.

In Finland, cereal soups and porridges used to have an important place on the menu because in the earlier days grains were the main source of nourishment. Cereal dishes were community meals, and a big porridge kettle in the middle of a long table created a feeling of well-being. With an improved standard of living, the use of cereals has diminished, but many nutritionists still emphasize the virtues of whole-grain dishes.

Even though the days of community meals are gone, there is still a certain warm and close-to-the-earth feeling about a bowl of hot cereal. Whole grains are a relatively good—and inexpensive—source of protein, and they provide vitamins and minerals that are especially valuable for those who are still growing.

There is one rule about cooking cereal: it should be done slowly—not by boiling, but by merely "hatching." Besides being gentle to the nutrients, this method brings out the full, strong flavors.

Cooking utensils. A double boiler is best for providing the right kind of low heat. But a heavy-bottomed saucepan will do if you keep the heat at a minimum. For stirring in flour, use a wire or twig whisk.

Method of cooking.   Sprinkle the cereal over hot liquid that is just about to reach the boiling point. With one hand, sprinkle the cereal; with the other, whisk vigorously to prevent lumps.

Simmer the mixture about 5 minutes, stirring and letting it thicken. Then lower the heat and hatch below the boiling point 20 to 50 minutes, depending on the cereal. While hatching, keep the pot tightly covered.

Milk-base cereals.   Don't add salt before the cereal is done, or else it may curdle. To prevent the milk from scorching, butter the bottom of the pan lightly.

One serving as specified in this book is considerably smaller than one serving in the old days. It is just enough for an adult who doesn't do physical labor, but a growing child may want a double portion.

Cereal Soups

These soups are mostly breakfast dishes, but some can also be eaten as dessert. Before serving, add a lump of butter and beat lightly; this will make it light and smooth. Use leftover soups as a base for pancakes. Add 1 or 2 eggs, beat, and fry in a pancake pan.

GRAHAM SOUP [GRAHAMVELLI]

3 cups skim milk   ½ teaspoon sea salt, or to taste
¼ cup graham (or whole wheat) flour

Bring the milk to the boiling point. Sprinkle the flour over the milk, beating well with a wire whisk to prevent lumps from forming.

Simmer 5 minutes, letting the soup thicken. Stir once in a while.

Turn the heat as low as possible. Cover the pot and let hatch about 10 minutes. Season with salt.

Serve for breakfast or for lunch. Add a lump of butter if you want.
Servings: 4.

VELVET SOUP [SAMETTIVELLI]

4 cups milk   ½ teaspoon sea salt, or to taste
4 tablespoons unbleached flour or   1 teaspoon raw sugar or honey
  barley flour   ¼ teaspoon vanilla extract
2 eggs

Bring 3 cups of milk to a boil. Mix the flour well with 1 cup of cold milk; beat out any lumps. Pour this mixture slowly into the hot milk, beating constantly with a wire whisk.

Simmer gently 10 minutes, beating all the time. The soup will become thick, smooth, and foamy.

Beat the eggs lightly in a bowl. Remove the soup from the heat. Pour some of the hot soup into the eggs, mix well, and then pour the egg mixture into the hot soup. Stir. Heat the soup, stirring all the time, but do not let it boil.

Remove from the heat and add salt, sugar or honey, and vanilla.

Serve warm or cold for breakfast or for dessert. Add a spoonful of strawberry jam.

Servings: 4 to 5.

OAT SOUP [KAURAVELLI]

This is the right food if you have an upset stomach: mild, but still nourishing. It's also one of the first foods given to a baby after mother's milk.

2 cups water	1-1/3 cups milk (skim or whole)
1/4–1/3 cup rolled oats	1/2 teaspoon sea salt, or to taste

Bring the water to a boil and sprinkle the oats over the water, beating with a wire whisk. Simmer 5 minutes, stirring. Add the milk, cover partially, and simmer 10 minutes.

Remove from the heat and season with salt.

Serve for breakfast, or at any time for someone with stomach trouble.

Servings: 4.

OAT AND PRUNE SOUP [KAURAKEITTO]

3 cups water	1/3 cup blanched almonds, slivered
10 pitted prunes	1 teaspoon sea salt, or to taste
1/2 cup rolled oats	1 teaspoon honey
1 cup milk	2 tablespoons cream

Soak the prunes in 3 cups of water until plump. Use the soaking water for the soup. Reserve the prunes.

Bring the water to a boil and sprinkle the oats over it, beating with a wire whisk. Simmer until the soup thickens, about 5 minutes. Lower the heat, cover, and hatch about 15 minutes. Put the soup through a sieve or blend in blender. Pour it back into the pan.

Add the milk and reheat. Throw in the prunes and almonds. Simmer about 5 minutes. Remove from the heat and add salt, honey, and cream.

Serve for breakfast or for dessert, warm or cold.

Servings: 4 to 6.

BARLEY FLOUR SOUP [OHRAJAUHOVELLI]

3 cups milk
¼ cup barley flour

½ teaspoon sea salt, or to taste
2 teaspoons butter

Bring the milk to a boil and sprinkle the flour over it, beating well with a wire whisk. Simmer 10 minutes, stirring all the time.

Remove from the heat; add salt and butter. Beat so that the soup becomes smooth and airy.

Serve for breakfast, or try it as an appetizer for an earthy meal.
Servings: 4.

BARLEY FLOUR AND APPLE SOUP [TERVEYSKEITTO]

2½ cups water
¼ cup barley flour
2 tart green apples, grated

1–2 tablespoons honey
¼ cup cream

Bring the water to a boil and sprinkle the flour over it, beating well with a wire whisk. Simmer, stirring, about 5 minutes, or until the soup thickens. Lower the heat to a minimum. Add the grated apples, cover, and simmer about 10 minutes.

Remove from the heat; add honey and cream. Cool. Chill before serving.

Serve chilled for breakfast or for dessert.
Servings: 4.

Porridges

Porridges, like soups, are breakfast, lunch, and dessert dishes. Especially suitable for desserts are the porridges that have been cooked in berry juice or mixed with fruit or preserves.

Porridges are served with a lump of butter or a spoonful of jam, and cold milk, or cream is poured over the porridge. Some porridges are good with sugar and cinnamon. Sometimes a cold dessert soup may be poured over warm or cold porridge and then served as dessert.

Leftover porridges can be sliced and fried in butter. They can also be mixed with milk and a couple of eggs and used as a pancake base. Barley, rice, or oatmeal porridge can be mixed into a meatloaf instead of bread crumbs.

GRAHAM PORRIDGE [GRAHAMPUURO]

2-2/3 *cups water*
  ½ *teaspoon sea salt, or to taste*
  ¾ *cup graham (or whole wheat)*
    flour

1–2 *tablespoons butter*

Bring the salted water to a boil and sprinkle the flour over it, beating well with a wire whisk. Simmer about 5 minutes, stirring once in a while with a wooden spoon.

Lower the heat to a minimum, cover the pot, and let hatch 15 to 20 minutes. Stir in the butter before serving.

Serve for breakfast either plain or with cold milk.
Servings: 4.

CRANBERRY-GRAHAM PORRIDGE [KARPALO-GRAHAMPUURO]

2-2/3 *cups cranberry juice*
  ¾ *cup graham (or whole wheat)*
    flour

3 *tablespoons honey, or to taste*
   (if unsweetened juice is used)
½ *teaspoon sea salt*

Heat the cranberry juice and whisk the flour in. Simmer, stirring, until the porridge thickens.

Lower the heat to a minimum, cover the pot, and hatch 20 minutes. Add honey and salt, if necessary.

Serve warm for breakfast or dessert. Cold cream can be poured over it.
Servings: 4.

POTATO PORRIDGE [PERUNAPUURO]

This is an old Western Finland dish. The flavors are earthy, with associations of the harvest season.

1 *lb potatoes*
4 *cups water*

1 *teaspoon sea salt, or to taste*
2/3 *cup rye or barley flour*

Boil the potatoes in their jackets until done. Reserve the cooking liquid.

Peel the potatoes and mash or put through a sieve. Add 3 cups of liquid and salt. Pour the mixture into a saucepan and heat. Sprinkle the flour into it, whisking well. Simmer 5 to 10 minutes. Lower the heat to a minimum, cover, and hatch. Rye flour requires 45 to 60 minutes; barley flour, 30 minutes.

Serve hot for breakfast or lunch. Add butter and milk.
Servings: 4 to 5.

OAT PORRIDGE [KAURAPUURO]

3 cups water   1 cup rolled oats
½ teaspoon sea salt, or to taste

Bring the salted water to a boil and sprinkle the oats in, stirring with a wooden spoon. Simmer about 5 minutes, or until it thickens.

Turn the heat to a minimum, cover, and hatch 15 to 25 minutes.

Serve hot for breakfast. Add a lump of butter and/or cold milk. Or pour some cold dessert soup over it.
Servings: 4.

AUTUMN PORRIDGE [SYYSPUURO]

2-2/3 cups water   ¼ teaspoon cinnamon
    1 cup rolled oats   ¼ teaspoon salt
    ¼ cup lingonberry or cranberry
        preserves

Bring the water to a boil and sprinkle the oats in, stirring with a wooden spoon. Simmer about 5 minutes, or until it thickens.

Turn the heat to a minimum; add the preserves, cinnamon, and salt. Hatch 15 to 25 minutes.

Serve warm for breakfast. Pour cold milk over it.
Servings: 4.

PEARL BARLEY PORRIDGE [OHRARYYNIPUURO]

2 cups water   1-1/3 cups milk
1 cup pearl barley   ½ teaspoon sea salt, or to taste

Rinse the barley and soak in water overnight. Pour the barley and water into a saucepan, bring to a boil, and simmer about 10 minutes.

Add the milk and simmer, partially covered, about 1 hour. Remove from the heat and season with salt.

Serve hot for breakfast or lunch. Add a lump of butter and cold milk. Leftover porridge is very good when fried.
Servings: 4.

BARLEY FLOUR-BLUEBERRY PORRIDGE
[OHRA-MUSTIKKAPUURO]

2-2/3 cups water   1–2 tablespoons raw sugar or honey
    ¾ cup barley flour   ½ teaspoon sea salt
    ½ cup fresh or frozen blueberries

Bring the water to a boil and sprinkle the barley flour over it, beating well with a wire whisk. Simmer 5 minutes, or until the porridge thickens, stirring well.

Lower the heat to a minimum. Add the blueberries, cover the pot, and hatch 20 to 25 minutes. Add sugar or honey and salt.

Serve hot for breakfast with cold milk or cream.
Servings: 4.

BUTTERMILK PORRIDGE [PIIMÄPUURO]

This tastes a little like pumpkin pie and is a real energy bomb to start a day.

2-2/3 cups buttermilk
¾ cup barley flour
¼ cup blackstrap or ordinary
  molasses

½ teaspoon sea salt, or to taste
¼ teaspoon cinnamon

Add the flour to the buttermilk and beat well. Heat slowly, in a double boiler, taking care not to let it boil. Cover and hatch 20 minutes. Stir a couple of times while cooking.

Season with molasses, salt, and cinnamon.

Serve warm for breakfast with cold milk.
Servings: 4.

RYE PORRIDGE [RUISPUURO]

2-2/3 cups water
½ teaspoon sea salt, or to taste

¾ cup rye flour

Bring the salted water to a boil and whisk in the rye flour. Simmer about 5 minutes.

Lower the heat to a minimum, cover, and hatch 1 hour.

Serve hot for breakfast or lunch, with a lump of butter.
Servings: 4.

RYE-CRANBERRY PORRIDGE [RUIS-KARPALOPUURO]

2-2/3 cups cranberry juice (ordinarily   ½ teaspoon sea salt
    lingonberry is used)   3 tablespoons raw sugar or honey
    ¾ cup rye flour   (if unsweetened juice is used)

Heat the juice and whisk in the flour. Simmer 5 minutes, or until the porridge
thickens. Do not let boil.

Lower the heat to a minimum, cover, and hatch 1 hour. Add salt and sugar or
honey, if needed.

Serve warm for breakfast with cold milk.
Servings: 4.

RICE PORRIDGE [RIISIPUURO]

Rice porridge is Christmas porridge. One blanched almond is hidden in the
Christmas porridge to bring the finder happiness in the coming year.

1½ cups water   2 cups milk
    1 cup rice (see Note)   ½ teaspoon sea salt, or to taste

Use a double boiler. Heat the water, add rice, and cover the pot. Bring to a boil
and simmer about 20 minutes, or until most of the water is absorbed.

Add the milk, lower the heat to a minimum, and partially cover the pot. Hatch
until the milk has been absorbed and the rice has turned into thick porridge.
Before serving, season with salt.

When served warm, cinnamon and sugar are often sprinkled over the top.
When served cold, juice soup is often poured over the porridge for a dessert.

Note: White rice is ordinarily used for this because it easily turns into porridge.
If brown rice is used, it takes much longer, up to 1½ hours.
Servings: 4.

OVEN RICE PORRIDGE [UUNI-RIISIPUURO]

2 cups milk   1 teaspoon sea salt
1 cup water   2 tablespoons butter
1 cup white or brown rice

Preheat the oven to 250°F. In a saucepan, combine the milk and water and heat
the mixture until almost boiling. Use half of the butter to grease an ovenproof pot or
casserole. Pour the rice and salt into the pot. Pour the scalded liquid over it. Drop
the rest of the butter in.

Bake, uncovered, about 1 hour. Then lower the heat to 200°F, and hatch 1½ to 2
hours more. The porridge is ready when all liquid has disappeared and the
porridge is firm. There should be a brown coating on the top.

Another method: Use barley instead of rice.

Serve warm with butter. Eat for breakfast, lunch, or dessert. Fry leftovers.
Servings: 4.

BUCKWHEAT PORRIDGE [TATTARIPUURO]

3 cups water
1 teaspoon sea salt, or to taste

¾ cup cracked buckwheat (kasha)
1 tablespoon butter

Bring the salted water to a boil and stir in the buckwheat. Simmer about 10 minutes, or until it has absorbed some water.

Lower the heat to a minimum, cover, and let hatch until the porridge is done, about ½ hour. (Some buckwheat takes longer, up to 1 hour.)

Add butter and/or milk.
Servings: 4.

OVEN BUCKWHEAT PORRIDGE [TATTARI-UUNIPUURO]

1½ cups whole buckwheat
1½ teaspoons sea salt, or to taste

4 tablespoons butter
Water to cover

Roast the buckwheat in a hot, greaseless frying pan. Use a heavy pan; do not burn.

Preheat the oven to 250°F. Pour the buckwheat into an ovenproof deep pot. Add salt and butter. Pour just enough water over the buckwheat to cover. Cover the pot and bake ½ hour. Remove the cover and bake until all the liquid has been absorbed, the porridge is done, and the top has browned—about 2 hours.

Servings: 4 to 6.

FRIED PORRIDGE [PAISTETTU PUURO]

Leftover cold porridge

Butter

Slice the cold porridge thickly and fry it in butter. Fry rather slowly to get a thick, brown, crisp crust on the porridge slices. Rice, barley, and buckwheat porridges are especially tasty this way.

Chapter 2

APPETIZERS AND SMORGASBORD DISHES
[ALKURUUAT JA VOILEIPÄPÖYTÄRUUAT]

The famous Scandinavian smorgasbord tradition prevails also in Finland, where it is called *voileipäpöytä*. Smorgasbord dining is common to all restaurants and festivals, and one attacks a large smorgasbord with a determined mood of indulgence and a knowledge that this is not done every day! Parties are often arranged in the smorgasbord style.

A smorgasbord starts with the cold table; there are numerous fish, meat, and salad dishes, all appetizingly arranged on trays. Freshness and quality are emphasized. The hot courses are usually presented on a smaller side table, which says something about their importance. After 4 or 5 helpings from the cold table, one can't be expected to take the warm meatballs and casseroles very seriously!

In ordinary restaurant eating, a familiar item on the menu is *leikkelelautanen*, a cold-cut plate. It consists of a few assorted smorgasbord dishes. Usually there are cold meats, salted fish, smoked fish, salad, and hard-boiled eggs cut in half and covered with pieces of herring or anchovy. The plate is served with potatoes; although it is meant to be a first course, it is often a sufficient lunch by itself.

In everyday eating at home, a miniature smorgasbord often starts the meal. It is eaten from the same plate as the main dish and is not considered a separate course. It may consist of canned herring, shoemaker's salmon, or some other inexpensive favorite, and is served with the same boiled potatoes that then accompany the main dish.

Make your own cold-cut plate or smorgasbord by using any of the recipes given in this section. Some dishes are common in all Scandinavian countries, and some are characteristically Finnish. The Finnish smorgasbord is not as fancy and does not have the rich mayonnaise dressings and decorations that the Danish one has, for example.

The division of foods into separate courses is not very important in Finnish eating. Many of the smorgasbord dishes can be served by themselves. Friends are often invited over for "a little something" (instead of dinner), and one of these smorgasbord dishes is often served.

ITALIAN SALAD [ITALIANSALAATTI]

I don't know why it's called "Italian"—the taste is mellow, with a touch of tartness. This salad is traditionally a Sunday treat.

½ lb cooked veal, tongue, or ham, sliced and cut into small cubes
1 large boiled potato, cut into small cubes
2 boiled carrots, cut into small cubes

1 tart apple, peeled, cored, and cut into small cubes
1 cup fresh or frozen peas
1 small dill pickle, cut into small cubes

Dressing:
1 egg yolk
½ teaspoon prepared mustard
¼ teaspoon grated horseradish
1/3 cup oil
1 tablespoon lemon juice

¼ teaspoon sea salt
⅛ teaspoon pepper
1 teaspoon ice water
¼ cup heavy cream, whipped

Mix together all of the cubed ingredients and the peas.

To make the dressing, in a narrow-bottomed mixing bowl, beat the egg yolk, mustard, and horseradish. Pour in half of the oil, drop by drop, stirring vigorously all the time with a wooden spoon. In this way the mixture won't curdle.

Add the lemon juice, beat well, and start adding the rest of the oil. Now you can pour the oil a little faster, but be sure to stir well all the time. Add salt, pepper, and ice water. Beat well. Water will make the dressing shinier. Fold in the whipped cream.

Combine the salad and dressing; mix well. Chill the salad. Allow a few hours for the tastes to blend; overnight is even better.

As an appetizer, serve on a lettuce leaf in cocktail glasses. On a smorgasbord, serve the salad in a large bowl and double the recipe. As hors d'oeuvres, fill small ripe cherry tomatoes with the salad. Or serve as an Italian Salad Sandwich (see page 35).
Servings: 4 to 6 as an appetizer.

FISH SALAD [KALASALAATTI]

1 lb leftover boiled or smoked fish
¼ cup chopped fresh dill leaves

Bibb lettuce leaves

Dressing:

3 tablespoons sour cream
1 teaspoon prepared mustard
1 cup yogurt or viili (see page 187)

Salt to taste, if necessary
¼ cup finely chopped chives

Bone the fish and remove all skin. Break it into fork-size bites. Mix in the dill. Put the lettuce leaves into cocktail glasses and place the fish on the lettuce. Chill.

For the dressing, mix together the sour cream and mustard. Fold in the yogurt or viili and season with salt and chives. Pour the dressing over the salad.

Serve chilled as an appetizer. Or make one large salad by pouring the dressing over and serving on a smorgasbord.

Servings: 4 to 6.

WEST COAST SALAD [LÄNSIRANNIKON SALAATTI]

A popular dish in all the Scandinavian countries, this salad is found on almost every restaurant's smorgasbord.

1 cup asparagus tips, fresh or
　canned
1 cup sliced mushrooms, fresh or
　canned
¾ lb seafood (usually a combination
　of cooked small shrimp, crabmeat,
　crayfish meat, and mussels)

1 large ripe tomato, cut into cubes
1/3 cup chopped fresh dill leaves
1 cup shredded lettuce
4–6 whole lettuce leaves
2–3 hard-boiled eggs, cut into wedges
　A few whole dill leaves

Dressing:

3 tablespoons lemon juice or
　vinegar
5 tablespoons oil

¼–½ teaspoon sea salt
⅛ teaspoon white pepper
　Dash of sugar

If you use fresh asparagus and mushrooms, prepare them first. Boil the asparagus in lightly salted water until tender. Cool and cut into 1-inch pieces. Drop the mushrooms into boiling salted water for about 3 minutes. Drain well and cool.

Combine the seafood, asparagus, mushrooms, tomato, and dill. Mix together all of the dressing ingredients, shake well, and pour over the salad. Cover the bowl and chill 2 to 3 hours or overnight to let the dill taste blend through.

Before serving, toss in the shredded lettuce. Serve the salad on whole lettuce leaves in cocktail glasses. Decorate with wedges of hard-boiled eggs and sprigs of dill. Keep well chilled until serving time.

Another method: You may use only two or three kinds of the seafood listed above. It is also possible to use lobster chunks. The important thing is the dill flavor.

Serve as an appetizer. Or serve in a large bowl on a smorgasbord. The salad is a popular late-night snack with crisp toast, butter, and a well-chilled white wine.

Servings: 4 to 6.

SMOKED FISH SALAD [SAVUKALASALAATTI]

¼ European cucumber, cubed
6 radishes, cubed
¼ teaspoon sea salt
¾ lb smoked fish, boned and flaked
1 tart apple, peeled, cored, and cubed
1 large potato, boiled, peeled, and
  cubed

2 tablespoons chopped parsley
2 tablespoons chopped fresh dill
  leaves
2 tablespoons chopped chives

Dressing:
¼ cup mayonnaise

¼ cup sour cream

Sprinkle the cucumber and radish cubes with salt and let stand in the refrigerator
1 hour. Squeeze the excess water out. Mix all of the ingredients for the salad.

Mix together the mayonnaise and sour cream. Combine the dressing and the
salad. Toss well. Cover the bowl and let stand in the refrigerator at least 2 hours
before serving.

As an appetizer, serve on a lettuce leaf. As a luncheon dish or late-night snack,
serve with thin slices of toast or toasted rolls.
   Servings: 4 to 6 as an appetizer.

ROSOLLI, OR HERRING SALAD [ROSOLLI TAI SILLISALAATTI]

Although it's called herring salad, the herring is sometimes left out altogether.
The herring can be served separately for those who like it. *Rosolli* is a traditional
Christmas salad, but it is also served at other times.

2 cups cubed, boiled or pickled beets
1 cup cubed, boiled potatoes
1 cup cubed, boiled carrots
½ cup cubed dill pickle
2/3 cup cubed tart apple

1 small onion, chopped fine
½ teaspoon sea salt, if desired
¼ teaspoon white pepper, if desired
1–2 fillets of herring, cut into
  serving pieces

Dressing:
½ cup heavy cream, whipped

1 tablespoon white vinegar, dyed red
  with 1 slice of cooked beet

When you boil the vegetables, make sure that you do not cut the roots of the
beets—or the color will run out. Just to be on the safe side, boil the beets in a
separate kettle.

Mix together all of the salad ingredients except the herring. Chill a few hours or overnight to let the tastes blend. The longer the salad stands, the better.

Just before serving, whip the cream. Dye the vinegar by soaking the beet slice in it for a few minutes. Color the cream pink by adding the dyed vinegar. Mix well. Keep chilled until ready to serve. Do *not* combine with the salad.

Serve the salad as an appetizer or on a smorgasbord. Put it into a large glass salad bowl. Arrange the herring pieces on a separate serving dish. Serve the pink cream separately in a small glass bowl. Some people prefer the salad plain; others like to add either herring or dressing, or both.

Servings: 8 to 10.

MUSHROOM SALAD [SIENISALAATTI]

4 cups water	1 lb mushrooms, cleaned and sliced
1 teaspoon sea salt	½ teaspoon sea salt

Dressing:

½ cup sour cream	2 tablespoons grated onion, or to
½ teaspoon raw sugar	taste

Bring the salted water to a rolling boil. Drop in the mushrooms and let cook 2 to 3 minutes. Drain them well and pat dry. Chop the dried, cooled mushrooms very fine. Sprinkle with the ½ teaspoon of salt and let stand about 1 hour.

Combine the sour cream, sugar, and onion, and stir into the chopped mushrooms. Mix well. Cover the bowl and chill at least 2 hours, preferably overnight, to let the tastes blend thoroughly.

Serve the salad as an appetizer or from a large bowl on a smorgasbord.
Servings: 4 to 6.

VINEGARED SMELTS [ETIKKASILAKAT]

This dish reminds one of the Spanish delicacy *escabeche*, but it is clearly Scandinavian in seasonings—one of the truly superb fish appetizers.

4 tablespoons rye flour	½ lb cleaned small smelts, butter-
½ teaspoon sea salt	flied (See Note)
¼ teaspoon white pepper	1/3 cup oil (for frying)

Marinade:

1 cup white vinegar	½ teaspoon whole white peppercorns
½ teaspoon sea salt	1 bay leaf
1 tablespoon raw sugar or	
honey	

Filling:

1 small red onion, sliced thinly and	½ cup chopped fresh dill leaves
separated into rings	

Mix together in a bowl the rye flour, salt, and pepper. Dip the butterflied smelts into the mixture on both sides. Heat the oil in a heavy frying pan until very hot. Fry the fish quickly in the oil on both sides, less than 1 minute per side. The fish should be evenly browned and crisp. Drain well on paper towels.

Combine the ingredients for the marinade in a saucepan. Cover, bring to a boil, and simmer 5 minutes. Let cool a little.

In a glass bowl or wide-mouthed jar, arrange half the fish. On top of that, sprinkle a generous layer of chopped dill and red onion slices. Then use the remaining fish, dill, and onion. Pour the marinade over the top. Cover the bowl and refrigerate for 24 hours. Then it's ready to serve, but it will keep about 1 week.

Pour off most of the marinade. Serve as an appetizer or on a smorgasbord. Serve with tiny boiled potatoes (see page 106) or beet salad (see page 116).

Note: When butterflying the smelts, it is important to remove the backbone without tearing the flesh. Place your thumb in the stomach of the fish, all the way along the backbone. Loosen first the bones on one side by pulling gently towards the backbone, repeat for the other side. Pull the backbone out from the head end to the tail.
Servings: 4 to 6.

ROLLED SMELTS [SILAKKARULLAT]

The vinegar brings out the surprisingly bright colors of the fish skin: silver, blue, gold. The dish looks pretty and decorative.

½ *lb cleaned small smelts, butterflied*

Marinade:
 1 *cup water*
 ½ *cup white vinegar*
 1 *teaspoon raw sugar or honey*
 ½ *teaspoon sea salt*
 3 *whole allspice*
 3 *whole white peppercorns*
 ½ *bay leaf*

Decoration:
 Fresh dill sprigs

Roll the butterflied fish into tight little rolls skin side out, starting from the tail end. Put the rolls side by side into a shallow, flameproof kettle.

In a saucepan, combine the marinade ingredients. Cover, bring to a boil, and simmer 5 minutes. Pour the hot marinade over the fish rolls. Cover the kettle and simmer very gently about 10 minutes. To keep the heat low, uncover the kettle partially if necessary. Remove from the heat and let the fish cool in the marinade. Chill well before serving.

When the marinade cools, it will jell. You may serve the fish as is, or you may remove the rolls from the marinade and serve them on a glass platter. Decorate with fresh dill sprigs. Serve as an appetizer or on a smorgasbord.
Servings: 4 to 6.

SHOEMAKER'S SALMON [SUUTARINLOHI]

The name of this dish indicates that it is one of the most popular and appreciated everyday appetizers. It is served in Finnish homes before a weekday dinner as a miniature smorgasbord with some hot boiled potatoes.

½ lb cleaned small smelts, butterflied	½–1 teaspoon sea salt, or to taste

Marinade:

1 small onion, chopped	1 teaspoon raw sugar or honey
2/3 cup white vinegar	¼ teaspoon allspice
¼ cup water	

Use a wide-mouthed glass jar or a deep, small glass bowl with an even bottom. Arrange the fish fillets in the bowl in layers, skin side down, and sprinkle each layer with salt.

Combine the marinade ingredients in a saucepan, cover, and simmer 5 minutes. Pour the hot marinade over the fish. Cover the bowl and refrigerate for 1 to 2 days.

Serve either as an appetizer or on a smorgasbord with boiled potatoes.
Servings: 4 to 6.

GLASSMASTER'S HERRING [LASIMESTARINSILLI]

This is probably the most popular pickled herring dish. It is eaten in fancy restaurants as well as with simple meals at home.

1 small salted herring, soaked if necessary	2 small onions, sliced thin
1–2 carrots, sliced thin	A few shavings of horseradish
	1 teaspoon mustard seeds

Marinade:

1½–2 cups wine vinegar	5 whole cloves
5 whole allspice	2–3 whole bay leaves
½ cup raw sugar	

Clean the herring, but do not skin or fillet. Cut it into steaks about 1 inch thick. Put the herring pieces into a wide-mouthed glass jar, alternating layers with the carrot and onion slices, mustard seeds, and horseradish. (Do not use much horseradish, or the herring will become bitter.)

In a saucepan, combine the ingredients for the marinade. Bring to a quick, rolling boil, and then simmer about 5 minutes. Cool. Pour the cold marinade over the herring. The herring must be completely covered. Close the jar and refrigerate for 1 or 2 days.

Serve as an appetizer or on a smorgasbord.
Servings: 4 to 6.

DECORATED HERRING [KORISTETTU SILLI]

Herring is always seen on Finnish menus—both in restaurants and in homes. Salted herring is a must on smorgasbords, served with different dressings and decorated in different ways. For these recipes, use either a whole salted herring or a canned, plain herring.

Whole salted herring is often soaked to achieve a milder taste. It should first be cleaned, but the boning and filleting should be done after soaking. Soak the whole herring in tea, milk, buttermilk, or light beer 3 to 5 hours. If it's very salty, it may be soaked for up to 12 hours.

After soaking, fillet the fish, remove the skin, and pick out any small bones. Cut it crosswise into fork-size pieces. The herring pieces are usually arranged on an oval glass herring plate in the shape of the fish. Use any of the following decorations:

I:

Chopped onion or chives   *Sour cream*

Cover the herring pieces with chopped onion or chives. Decorate with sour cream.

II:

½ cup mayonnaise   *1 tablespoon capers*
1 tablespoon finely chopped green   *1 hard-boiled egg, cut into wedges*
* olives*   *5–6 whole green olives*
1 tablespoon chopped parsley

Mix together the mayonnaise, chopped olives, parsley, and capers. Top the herring with this mixture. Decorate the dish with egg wedges and whole olives.

III:

2 tablespoons wine vinegar   *2 hard-boiled eggs, chopped*
2 tablespoons chopped fresh dill   *1 small dill pickle, chopped fine*
* leaves*   *1 pickled beet, chopped fine*
2 tablespoons chopped chives   *Sour cream*

Sprinkle the herring with vinegar. Place the fish on a round glass plate. Sprinkle with dill and chives. Arrange the eggs, pickles, and beets around the fish.

Serve with sour cream if desired.
Servings: 4 to 6.

SUGAR-SALTED SALMON [SOKERISUOLATTU LOHI]

This dish is also called "little-salted"; the delicious flavor of the salmon is kept by using a minimum amount of salt. It is one of the purest delicacies.

2 teaspoons coarse sea salt   *1 teaspoon crushed white peppercorns*
1 teaspoon raw sugar   *Fresh dill leaves (about 1 cup)*
2 salmon fillets (about 1 lb each)

Accompaniments:
Poached eggs
Lemon wedges
Fresh dill sprigs

Creamed spinach (see page 111)
Boiled new potatoes (see page 106)

Combine the salt and sugar. Sprinkle the fish with this mixture and pat it into the flesh lightly. Sprinkle with crushed peppercorns and cover the fish completely with dill leaves. Put the two fillets together, with the flesh sides together and the skin sides out. The tail end of one fillet should face the wider end of the other.

Wrap the fillets in freezer wrap. Make a tight package and put it into a shallow bowl. Put a light weight on top of the package. Let it stand in the refrigerator 1 day. (Although 1 day is considered best, it will keep 3 to 4 days.) Pour off any liquid that has formed. With a sharp knife, cut paper-thin slices.

Another method: Instead of using dill, try tiny sprigs of spruce.

Serve as an appetizer or on a smorgasbord. Arrange the fish slices on a serving platter. Surround them with poached eggs, lemon wedges, and fresh dill sprigs. In separate bowls, serve creamed spinach and boiled potatoes. Although this dish is considered an appetizer, it is also perfect for a light and elegant main course, or for a late-night snack.

Iced schnapps (see page 197) and mineral water or a chilled white wine is usually served with salmon.

Servings: 8 to 10.

FISHERMAN'S FRESH SALTED FISH
[SAARISTOLAISITTAIN TUORESUOLATTU KALA]

This fish is much stronger in taste and saltier than the sugar-salted salmon. It originated in the Western Finnish archipelago.

3 cups water
3–4 tablespoons coarse sea salt
1 lb fresh fish, a fillet (salmon, bream, or whitefish)

6–8 whole fresh dill stalks, with leaves

Combine water and salt, and let the salt dissolve. To test for the correct saltiness, put an uncooked potato into the water. When it swims—that is, when it does not touch the bottom of the dish but swims underneath the surface—the water is salty enough.

Sink the fish fillet in the water and add the dill. No weight should be needed, since the fish should stay submerged. Put into the refrigerator. It will be ready in about 6 hours. This method will soften and salt the fish evenly. To serve, cut into slices.

Serve as an appetizer, on a smorgasbord, or on top of a sandwich.

Note: The Finns traditionally used clean seawater, with additional salt to taste. But since it is impossible to find water that would be clean enough, it is better to mix the salt water.

Servings: 6 to 8.

BROILED SALMON WINGS [PARILOIDUT LOHENEVÄT]

Some restaurants have this dish as the specialty on their smorgasbord. Although the dish is simple, the secret of it is the dark brown, almost burned surface.

1½–2 lbs salmon wings and other leftover pieces (see Note)	1 teaspoon coarse sea salt
	1/3 cup oil

The fish pieces must be broiled with an extremely high heat. With an open fire—a fireplace or even a gas flame—use a wire picnic grill. Or broil the fish on a barbecue grill. It is also possible to prepare it in a heavy iron frying pan or directly over the heater of an electric stove.

Sprinkle the fish lightly with salt and let stand for 10 to 15 minutes. Brush with oil on all sides.

If you cook the fish over an open fire, broil it on all sides until it becomes dark brown, almost burned.

If you use a frying pan or stove, throw some coarse salt on the pan or heater. The pan must be very hot; otherwise the fish will stick. Broil on all sides until the fish is dark brown.

The fish should be almost black, but not bitterly burned. The pieces should remain whole and be juicy inside. This can be achieved by broiling quickly.

Place the fish on a platter and serve as an appetizer or on a smorgasbord.
Note: The salmon wings are the fins with the adjacent muscles. Other leftover pieces—such as the trimmings—can also be used. Use all of the pieces that remain when the salmon is filleted.
Some stores sell lox trimmings and wings. However, they are sometimes too salty for this dish.
Servings: 4 to 6.

COLD DECORATED SALMON [KYLMÄ KORISTETTU LOHI]

2–3 lbs salmon (a whole piece or fillets)	1–2 teaspoons sea salt
2–3 cups water	3 whole allspice
10 whole, strong fresh dill stalks, leaves removed	

Fish jelly:

2 cups broth from boiled fish	1 envelope gelatin
2 egg whites, beaten stiff	

Dressing:

Yolks of 2 hard-boiled eggs	¼ teaspoon sea salt
1 teaspoon honey or raw sugar	1 tablespoon finely chopped fresh
1 teaspoon prepared Dijon or German mustard	dill leaves
1 tablespoon lemon juice	½ cup cream, whipped stiff

Decoration:

Lettuce leaves
Whites of 2 hard-boiled eggs,
   chopped
Fresh dill leaves, left whole
Tomato wedges

Lemon slices or wedges
Cucumber slices
Asparagus tips, boiled
Radish flowers

To poach the fish, put the salmon into a fish kettle, add the water, dill stalks, salt, and allspice. Bring the water to a gentle boil, then cover partially, and simmer over a low heat until done, 30 to 45 minutes. Do not let it boil or break apart. Lift the fish carefully onto a plate and let it cool. Remove the skin. Reserve the cooking liquid. Chill the fish until ready to serve.

To make the fish jelly, pour the broth from the fish saucepan and heat. Add the beaten egg whites, stir, and simmer 2 minutes. The whites will absorb the impurities and make the jelly clear. Pour the broth into another pot through a sieve, lined with cheesecloth. Soften the gelatin in a little cold water; pour it into the broth; and heat until the gelatin dissolves. Pour it into an ice cube tray and chill.

To make the dressing, mash the egg yolks with the honey or sugar, mustard, lemon juice, salt, and chopped dill. Whip the cream and fold in. Let stand a couple of hours in the refrigerator, for the tastes to blend.

To decorate the fish, use a long serving platter and prepare a bed of lettuce. Place the cold fish on it. Spoon the dressing over the fish and sprinkle with the chopped egg whites and dill leaves. Cut the fish jelly into small cubes and arrange around the fish, together with the tomato and lemon wedges, cucumber slices, asparagus tips, and radish flowers. Chill until serving time.

Serve as an appetizer or on a smorgasbord. It is fine for a cold main course in the summer. In that case, allow about ½ pound salmon per person.

Servings: 6 to 8 as an appetizer.

FISH ROE WITH TOAST [MÄTI JA PAAHTOLEIPÄ]

In Scandinavia, uncooked fish roe is considered a delicacy that competes with caviar. I always prefer the small-egged burbot roe to caviar. Whitefish roe and pike roe are also sought after. Rainbow trout roe is exported from Finland to other Scandinavian countries and the prices are high.

All fish roe can be prepared this way—find your own favorite. For this recipe, use a roe that has very small eggs because it blends better with the other ingredients. The taste, when everything is mixed, is creamy; even if you are suspicious of raw fish, give it a try!

1 lb fish roe
1 teaspoon sea salt
1 cup heavy cream, whipped
1 cup sour cream
3 tablespoons finely chopped onion,
   or to taste

1/8 teaspoon white pepper, or to taste
Thin slices of toast
Butter

Freeze the fresh fish roe for a day and then thaw it. With this method you won't have to salt it heavily to cure it. Lightly salted fish roe is much more delicious than salty roe. After thawing, put the bags of fish roe into a bowl. The best way to remove all of the veins and membranes is to beat the roe. For small amounts use a fork; for larger amounts, a beater. Remove any membranes that stick to the beater.

Now salt the roe, using about 1 teaspoon per pound. Keep beating until the roe becomes light and airy.

Whip the heavy cream and fold in the sour cream. Stir the creams into the fish roe. Season with chopped onion and pepper. The roe should have a distinct onion taste, but the onion should not overwhelm. The same with the pepper. Mix well. Chill about 1 hour before serving.

Serve as an appetizer with toast, or as an elegant light supper or late snack. Place the bowl of roe on cracked ice. To keep the thin, crisp slices of toast warm, put them in a basket and cover them with a napkin. Serve thin curly slices of butter. Spread the toast with butter and/or a generous helping of the fish roe mixture.

The perfect drink to accompany this dish is chilled schnapps (see page 197) with mineral water or beer. A well-chilled white wine also tastes good.

Servings: 4 to 6 (more on a smorgasbord).

BLINI WITH FISH ROE [LINNIT JA MÄTI]

In Finland traditional Russian *blini* are always served in February, when the delicious burbot roe is in season.

Blini:

1 tablespoon active dry yeast	*1 egg*
1/3 cup water	*1 teaspoon sea salt*
½ cup cream	*2/3 cup boiling milk*
¾ cup buckwheat flour	*1 tablespoon melted butter*
¼ cup unbleached white flour	

Accompaniments:

½–¾ lb salted fish roe (see above)	*½ cup hot melted butter*
½ cup finely chopped onion	*Salt and pepper*
1 cup sour cream	

Dissolve the yeast in warm water in a medium-size bowl. Add the cream and whisk in the buckwheat flour and unbleached white flour. Put the bowl in a warm place and let stand 5 to 6 hours or overnight. The batter will bubble and become sour.

To make the pancakes, use a special blini pan or a crêpe pan. The blini pan is about the same size, but it has higher sides. Beat the egg and then beat it into the blini batter. Add the salt and beat in the boiling milk. For thicker blini, beat the yolk and white separately, and then fold in.

Fry the blini on both sides in a hot, buttered pan. They should be thick and brown. Turn carefully, so that they won't break. Keep hot until ready to serve. Blini are best when served directly from the pan.

As an appetizer or late-night snack, serve blini with fish roe or caviar. Put the salted fish roe in a small glass bowl. Use separate bowls for the chopped onion, sour cream and hot melted butter. Put a little of each on the blini, and season with salt and pepper. One blini per person as an appetizer should be enough. Serve with chilled schnapps (see page 197) and mineral water, or with a chilled white wine.

I have also served blini for breakfast, with just sour cream or some tart jam.
Servings: 4 to 6.

JELLIED PORK [PORSAANHYYTELÖ]

2 lbs lean, boneless pork (shoulder or butt), in one piece	3 whole cloves
	1 bay leaf
6 cups cold water	¼ teaspoon ground ginger, or 1 piece
1½ teaspoons sea salt	fresh ginger
3 whole allspice	2 envelopes gelatin
6 whole white peppercorns	¼ cup cold water

Decoration:
2 hard-boiled eggs   ½ cup cooked green peas,
                                              fresh or frozen

To boil the pork, bring the water, salt, and spices to a boil, cover, and simmer 5 minutes. Remove from the heat and cool a little. Put the whole piece of pork in the water, return to the heat, and bring to a boil. Cover the pot, lower the heat, and simmer slowly until the pork is done—about 1½ hours. Remove the meat from the broth and drain. Refrigerate the broth and skim off any fat from the surface.

Chop the cooled pork into tiny cubes. As molds for the jellied pork, use small cups or decorative little molds, rinsed with cold water. At the bottom of each cup, put one slice of hard-boiled egg and some peas. Fill the cup about ¾ full with the pork cubes.

Heat the broth and remove the spices. You will need about 4 cups of broth, so if there is more, simmer it for a while to reduce the amount. Soften the gelatin in ¼ cup cold water, add to the warm broth, and let the gelatin dissolve. Remove from the heat and let it cool just until it starts to set.

Pour the thickened liquid over the pork and stir a little. Chill until set. Before serving, remove the jellies from the molds.

Dressing (optional):
½ teaspoon raw sugar or honey   ½ teaspoon dry mustard
1 teaspoon vinegar, dyed with 1 slice ¼ teaspoon sea salt
  of raw or cooked beet   ¼ cup cream, whipped

Mix together the sugar or honey, vinegar, mustard, and salt. Fold in the whipped cream. Chill.

Serve as an appetizer on salad greens. Use dressing or lemon juice. Garnish with pickled beets (see page 117).
Yield: 6 to 8 small pork jellies.

JELLIED VEAL [VASIKANHYYTELÖ]

An excellent diet dish—light and high in protein. It can also be used as a cold cut to top sandwiches.

5 cups water	2 lbs boneless veal (butt, neck, or
1 carrot, scraped	shoulder), in one piece
1 bay leaf	2 tablespoons white vinegar
3 whole allspice	1 envelope gelatin
1 teaspoon sea salt	¼ cup cold water
4 whole white peppercorns	

Put the water, carrot, bay leaf, allspice, salt, and peppercorns into a kettle, and heat. Put the whole piece of meat in the water and bring to a boil slowly. Cover and simmer gently until the meat is done, a little more than 1 hour.

Remove the meat, let it cool, and chop very fine. Drain the seasonings from the broth and add the vinegar. Soften the gelatin in cold water and pour it into the warm broth. Let it dissolve. Put the chopped meat back into the broth and let stand 5 minutes.

Rinse a 2-quart loaf pan with cold water, and pour the veal mixture into it. Refrigerate to set. Unmold before serving.

Serve the whole loaf on a smorgasbord, decorated with lettuce leaves, cucumber slices, and lemon wedges. Or serve already sliced as an appetizer. Use lemon juice as a dressing.

Servings: 6 to 8.

BOILED TONGUE [KEITETTY KIELI]

1 beef tongue	1 onion, peeled and quartered
4–5 cups water	5 whole allspice
1 tablespoon sea salt	

Rinse the tongue first with cold water, then with hot water, and dry with paper towels. Bring the water, salt, onion, and allspice to a boil, and put the tongue in it. Cover and simmer about 2 hours, or until done.

Remove the tongue from the liquid. Skin while still hot and let cool. To serve, slice it thin as a cold cut.

Dressing:
Use this dressing when the tongue is served on a smorgasbord.

2 tablespoons white vinegar	½ teaspoon cinnamon
4 tablespoons grated horseradish	½ cup heavy cream, whipped
1 tablespoon raw sugar or honey	

Mix together the vinegar, horseradish, sugar or honey, and cinnamon. Fold in the whipped cream and mix. Chill.

On a smorgasbord, arrange the tongue slices either flat or rolled up on a tray. Put the dressing in a separate small bowl, which you can set in the middle of the tray. Decorate the tray with pickled onions (see page 118) and sprigs of parsley.
Servings: 10 or more on a smorgasbord.

LIVER PÂTÉ [MAKSAPASTEIJA]

1 lb ground pork or beef liver
¼ lb ground pork
1 onion, chopped fine
¼ cup melted butter
½ cup bread crumbs
½ cup cream or milk
2 eggs, beaten lightly

1 teaspoon marjoram leaves
½ teaspoon tarragon leaves
½ teaspoon white pepper
¼ teaspoon ground cloves
1 teaspoon sea salt
2 tablespoons Madeira

Mix the ground liver and pork. Brown the chopped onion in the butter and let cool. Soak the bread crumbs in the cream or milk and add to the liver mixture. Add the browned onion and butter. Stir in the eggs. Grind the marjoram and tarragon leaves in a mortar, and add them to the mixture with white pepper, cloves, salt, and Madeira.

Preheat the oven to 400°F. Grease well a 2-quart loaf pan and pour the liver mixture into it. The pan should not be completely full because the loaf expands. Put the loaf pan into a larger ovenproof pan, and fill the larger pan with water. Bake about 1 hour. Let cool in the pan. Before serving, remove the pâté from the pan. It can be frozen.

On a smorgasbord, place the whole pâté on a long serving platter. Decorate with lettuce, boiled whole prunes, cucumbers, and parsley. As an appetizer, cut a slice for each person, decorate, and serve on a small plate. You may also use the pâté as a cold cut and top sandwiches with it.
Servings: 10 or more on a smorgasbord.

Chapter 3

OPEN-FACE SANDWICHES
[VOILEIVÄT]

Sandwiches in Finland mean open-face sandwiches. Most of the sandwiches included here are well-known, the kind you will find in restaurants and cafes. Some of them I have had at friends' homes as an after-sauna meal; both cold and warm sandwiches are often served at that time, with cold beer or tea.

Cold Sandwiches

Large-size cold sandwiches are served as a light lunch dish, together with milk or beer. Smaller sandwiches are an excellent first course. And bite-size sandwiches—round or triangle—are served as cocktail snacks.

EGG-ANCHOVY SANDWICH [MUNA-ANJOVISLEIPÄ]

This is a well-known salty snack for a morning hangover. It is also a good lunch dish, with a glass of milk or beer.

One sandwich:

1 slice dark rye or whole wheat
  bread
1 teaspoon butter

1 hard-boiled egg, sliced
2–3 anchovies, preferably Scandinavian
  Dash of white pepper

Butter the bread and top with a row of egg slices. Put the anchovies on top. Sprinkle with pepper.

Another method: For little cocktail snacks, the egg-anchovy combination is good on top of Finn Crisps.

EGG-SALMON SANDWICH [MUNA-LOHIVOILEIPÄ]

This sandwich looks light and delicate and tastes the same. In a smaller size it makes an elegant cocktail sandwich.

One sandwich:

1 thin slice white or whole wheat
  bread
1 teaspoon sour cream
1–2 slices lightly salted salmon (see
  page 22)

1 egg, fried sunny-side up
  Dash of white pepper
  Dash of salt
1 lemon slice
1–2 fresh dill sprigs

Spread the bread with sour cream. Arrange the salmon slices on it. Top with the egg and dust lightly with salt and pepper. Garnish with lemon slice and dill sprigs.

Another method: For a small sandwich, cut out a little round slice of bread with a cookie cutter. Roll up the salmon slice; insert a toothpick through the roll and add a little piece of lemon. Cover the edges with dill sprigs.

EGG-BUTTER SANDWICH [MUNAVOI-VOILEIPÄ]

In the Finnish countryside, lunch baskets used to be filled with egg-butter sandwiches at harvest time to take to the fields. These sandwiches were a nourishing and satisfying treat after hard work, and today they bring back the same memories.

One sandwich:

1 hard-boiled egg, chopped
1 tablespoon butter, softened
1/8 teaspoon sea salt

1/8 teaspoon white pepper, or less
1 slice of bread
1 teaspoon chopped parsley

Mash together the chopped egg, softened butter, salt, and pepper. Spread the bread with it. Sprinkle with parsley.

ITALIAN SALAD SANDWICH [ITALIANSALAATTIVOILEIPÄ]

One sandwich:
1 slice light rye or whole wheat
  bread
½ teaspoon butter
1 lettuce leaf (usually Bibb lettuce)

½ cup Italian salad (see page 16)
1 thin orange slice
Sprig of parsley

Spread the bread with butter. Cover with lettuce leaf and arrange the salad on top. Decorate with orange slice and parsley.

Italian salad is considered a Sunday treat, so there is a special aura about the sandwich. Serve it as a luncheon dish or make smaller sandwiches for an appetizer.

LIVER PÂTÉ SANDWICH [MAKSAPASTEIJAVOILEIPÄ]

The combination of dark bread and liver pâté is one of the best! It's also one of the healthiest.

One sandwich:
1 slice of dark rye, whole rye, or
  buttermilk loaf (see page 152)
1 teaspoon butter or mayonnaise
1 thick slice liver pâté (see page 29)

1 boiled prune, split in half
2 slices dill pickle
3 cocktail onions
1 sprig parsley

Spread the bread with butter or mayonnaise. Top with the liver pâté slice. Garnish with prune, pickle slices, onions, and parsley.

SANDWICH CAKE [VOILEIPÄKAKKU]

Sandwich cakes were introduced to compete with all the sweets at coffee parties. They are now popular at buffets: weddings, christenings, and other receptions. They are easy to make, although this one requires a little patience.

1 large rectangular loaf of rye or
  whole wheat bread

Make the cake the day before you will serve it. Use bread that has been baked in a 2-quart loaf pan; if you buy the bread, get a loaf about the same size. Remove the crust from the bread and trim the bread to make a neat rectangle. Slice it lengthwise into 4 equally thick, long slices.

Prepare 3 fillings:

Filling I:

3 oz ham, chopped fine	1 tablespoon grated apple
1 oz butter, softened	1 teaspoon grated onion
2 tablespoons sour cream	1 tablespoon grated horseradish
1 teaspoon prepared mustard	1/4 teaspoon white pepper

Combine all of the ingredients to make a paste.

Filling II:

2 hard-boiled eggs, chopped	1/2 teaspoon dry mustard
1 tablespoon chopped leek or onion	1/4 teaspoon white pepper
2 tablespoons mayonnaise	Salt to taste

Combine all of the ingredients to make a paste.

Filling III:

4 oz smoked fish, boned and flaked	1 teaspoon chopped fresh dill
2 tablespoons sour cream	1 teaspoon chopped chives

Combine all of the ingredients to make a paste.

To assemble the cake, spread a layer of filling on 3 slices of the bread, 1 filling to a slice, and place the slices on top of each other to make a loaf. Put the fourth slice of bread on top. Do not let any filling come out from the sides. Keep the shape of the loaf as regular as possible. Press lightly.

Wet a few sheets of paper towel with cold water, wring them out, and wrap the cake tightly in the damp towel. Wrap aluminum foil around this. Put the package in the refrigerator overnight or for 24 hours.

Unwrap the package. Put the cake on a long serving platter. Cover with topping.

Topping:

3 oz Roquefort cheese, crumbled	1 tablespoon each: chopped parsley,
2 oz butter, softened	chopped dill, and chopped chives
3 tablespoons sour cream	Several drops of Tabasco sauce
3 tablespoons mayonnaise	(optional)

Combine all of the topping ingredients. Spread over the top and sides of the cake to cover it completely. On top and around the cake, arrange rolls of ham, cooked shrimp, thin slices of European cucumber, cherry tomatoes, and parsley. Keep the cake chilled until serving time.

Serve it whole on a buffet table, or cut it into slices and serve as an appetizer. **Servings:** 8 to 10.

Warm Sandwiches

Warm open-face sandwiches are either baked in the oven or broiled. Some of them—such as the cheese sandwiches—are served the same way as cold sandwiches. But the heartier ones, especially the steak sandwiches, are quite suitable for a main dinner course.

SMOKED FISH-SCRAMBLED EGG SANDWICH
[SAVUKALA-MUNAKOKKELIVOILEIPÄ]

One sandwich:

1 large slice rye or whole wheat bread
1 teaspoon butter

1 piece smoked fish, boned and flaked (2–3 oz)

Scrambled egg:

1 teaspoon butter
1 egg
1 tablespoon milk

1/8 teaspoon sea salt
1/8 teaspoon white pepper, or less
1 tablespoon chopped chives

Butter the bread. Place the flaked fish on half the slice. Set the oven at 200°F. Put the sandwiches in an oven pan and keep them warm until serving time.

To make the scrambled egg, melt the butter in a saucepan; beat the egg and milk lightly; and pour into the pan. Stir until the egg has cooked. Add salt, pepper, and chives. Spoon this on the other half of the sandwich.

SMOKED FISH SANDWICH [SAVUKALAVOILEIPÄ]

In Finland this sandwich is usually made of smoked Baltic herring, but it is also good with other kinds of fish.

4 slices bread
Butter

1 lb smoked fish, boned and flaked

Topping:

½ cup mayonnaise
2 tablespoons lemon juice
1/3 cup chopped fresh dill leaves

¼ teaspoon sea salt, or to taste
⅛ teaspoon white pepper
2 egg whites

Butter the slices of bread lightly and top with a thick layer of flaked fish.

Preheat the oven to 425°F. Combine the mayonnaise, lemon juice, dill, salt, and pepper. Beat the egg whites until hard and dry, and fold in the mayonnaise mixture. Mix quickly and spoon over the smoked fish.

The sandwiches should go into the oven as soon as possible so that the topping won't collapse. Bake 10 to 15 minutes, or until the tops are brown. Do not open the oven during the first 10 minutes.

Serve as a luncheon dish or as an evening snack. This sandwich is often served as an after-sauna meal with cold beer.
Servings: 4.

STEAK-MUSHROOM SANDWICH [PIHVI-SIENIVOILEIPÄ]

Since this dish is a whole meal, it is best served as a main dinner course. It is also fine for guests.

Mushroom sauce:

1½ cups fresh mushrooms
  1 tablespoon butter
  3 tablespoons unbleached white flour
  1 cup cream
  ¼ teaspoon sea salt
1/8 teaspoon white pepper
  Pinch of nutmeg
  ½ teaspoon dried dill, or 1 tablespoon chopped fresh dill (optional)

Steak mixture:

  2 tablespoons bread crumbs
  2 tablespoons cream
  1 small onion, chopped
  1 tablespoon butter
  2 lbs ground raw meat (preferably from a good cut)
  ½ teaspoon sea salt, or to taste
  ¼ teaspoon white pepper, or to taste
1/8 teaspoon allspice
  1 egg

  4 large slices of bread
  4 teaspoons butter

Decoration:

  Cucumber slices
  Tomato wedges
  Boiled asparagus
  Parsley

To make the mushroom sauce, chop the mushrooms and cook them in the butter in a saucepan until they become limp, 5 to 10 minutes. Do not brown. Sprinkle the flour over the mushrooms, stir, and cook about 3 minutes. Pour the cream into the saucepan very slowly, stirring well and bringing the mixture to a boil after each addition. Simmer the sauce about 5 minutes, or until it is thick and creamy. Remove from the heat and add seasonings. Set aside.

To make the steaks, soak the bread crumbs in the cream in a mixing bowl. Fry the chopped onion in butter and cool a little. Mix together the ground meat, bread crumb mixture, onion, salt, pepper, allspice, and egg. Knead well until it starts to stick to your hands. Divide into 4 equal parts.

Preheat the oven to 450°F. Butter the slices of bread. Make thick bread-sized patties from the meat mixture and cover the slices of bread. Be sure to cover the corners of the bread so they won't burn. Bake the sandwiches in the oven 10 to 15 minutes (15 minutes for well done). Remove from the oven. Turn up the broiler until it is quite hot.

Spoon the mushroom sauce over the steaks. Put the sandwiches under the broiler for 3 to 5 minutes, or until the tops have browned. Keep warm until served. Decorate with vegetables and parsley.

A light clear soup or a crisp salad would make an ideal first course.
Servings: 4.

KIDNEY SANDWICH [MUNUAISVOILEIPÄ]

This recipe dates from at least the turn of the century. It's truly delicious: try it even if you don't especially care for kidneys.

2 fresh lamb kidneys, or 1 beef
 kidney
1 tablespoon butter
2 tablespoons bread crumbs
⅛ teaspoon sea salt, or to taste

⅛ teaspoon white pepper
2 tablespoons lemon juice
2 egg yolks
4 large, thin slices of toasted bread
2 tablespoons chopped parsley

Clean the kidneys, and remove all of the fat and the membranes. Chop the kidneys very fine. Fry them quickly in butter and continue chopping in the pan. Then lower the heat a little and add the bread crumbs. Stir, and add salt, pepper, lemon juice, and egg yolks. Stir well and cook 2 to 3 minutes.

Spread the slices of toast with this paste. Sprinkle with parsley. Keep warm until served.
Servings: 4.

HAM AND CHEESE SANDWICH [KINKKU-JUUSTOVOILEIPÄ]

One sandwich:

1 large slice bread, preferably rye
½ teaspoon butter
1 teaspoon mustard
1 thick slice of ham, preferably
 smoked

1–2 thick slices of Swiss cheese or
 Gruyere
1 slice tomato
1 teaspoon chopped parsley

Spread the bread with butter and then mustard. Cover with ham and top with cheese.

Put the sandwich under the broiler until it starts to bubble and browns a little, 3 to 5 minutes. Take out and place tomato slice on top the cheese. Return to broiler for 1 to 2 minutes more. Garnish with chopped parsley. Serve immediately.

Serve as an evening snack—this is a typical after-sauna dish; great with cold beer!

CHEESE SANDWICH [JUUSTOVOILEIPÄ]

1 egg, beaten
2 tablespoons butter, softened
½ cup grated cheese (any strong
   cheese)

1 tablespoon mustard
⅛ teaspoon white pepper
   Salt, if necessary
4 slices bread

To the softened butter, add the grated cheese, mustard, pepper, and salt. Mix well. Add to the beaten egg.

Spread the slices of bread with this mixture. Put the sandwiches under the broiler for 5 to 8 minutes, or until nicely browned on top. Serve immediately.

Serve with summer soup (see page 53), nettle soup (see page 54), or other vegetable soups.

Servings: 4.

Chapter 4

SOUPS
[KEITOT]

Finnish soups are hearty, satisfying whole meals, to be eaten with slices of fresh bread. Most of these soups can be made very inexpensively; many of them use leftover meat and bones.

Fish Soups

These soups tend to be rather stew-like, rich and tasty; they are usually eaten as the main course at dinner. The fresher the fish, the stronger the taste and the better the soup. The salmon soups are delicacies that can be served as appetizers before dinner.

FISH BROTH [KALALIEMI]

2 lbs small, cleaned fish, with the
  heads, bones, and fins left in (see
  Note)
6 cups water
1 small piece celery root, or ⅛
  teaspoon celery seed
1 small parsnip, split in half
1 small red onion, halved
1 tablespoon sea salt, or to taste

1 bay leaf
5 whole allspice
10 whole white peppercorns
2 whole cloves
¼ cup finely chopped parsley
1/3 cup finely chopped dill
  leaves
Pinch of thyme
1 teaspoon raw sugar (optional)

Put the fish into a soup kettle. Pour the cold water over them, and add celery, parsnip, onion, salt, bay leaf, allspice, peppercorns, and cloves. Bring to a slow boil, cover, and simmer partially covered for 2 hours.

Strain, pressing on the pulp to squeeze out all the broth. Discard the pulp. Add the parsley, dill, and thyme. Add sugar, if used. Cover and let stand a few minutes before serving.

Serve as an appetizer soup. It is possible to thicken the soup with egg yolk, but this is not necessary.

Note: Use small fish such as perch or whiting, or a combination of several. Whiting makes a pleasantly mild broth.

Servings: 6.

FISH SOUP, FISHERMAN STYLE [KALASTAJAN KALAKEITTO]

This soup is best when made of very fresh sea fish. These have the strongest taste. Be sure to use enough fish. Leave the heads and bones in the soup; they add flavor.

1 teaspoon coarse sea salt, or
  to taste
3½–4 cups water
6 white peppercorns
3 whole allspice
1 large onion, peeled and
  quartered
6–8 small new potatoes in their
  jackets, halved or quartered

2 lbs cleaned fresh fish, cut into
  serving pieces
1 thick slice sour rye bread,
  buttered
½ cup chopped fresh dill leaves
¼ cup chopped chives
1 stick fresh butter, or less
Pinch of thyme

Bring the salted water to a boil in a soup kettle. Add the peppercorns, allspice, and onion. Cover and simmer 10 minutes. Add the potatoes, cover, and simmer over medium heat until the potatoes are done, about 20 minutes.

Add the fish pieces on top of the potatoes and lower the heat. On top of the fish, place a buttered slice of sour rye bread. It will provide a nice taste when it breaks. Cover the pot and simmer until the fish is done, about 30 minutes.

Remove what is left of the bread slice. Add the dill and chives, and stir in the butter. Check the salt. Cover and let stand for a little while to let the tastes blend. Add a tiny pinch of thyme. Reheat before serving if necessary.

Serve as a main course with good bread. Save the fish heads in the soup for those who like them: some prefer the eyes and some like the tiny delicate cheek muscle.

Servings: 4 to 6.

FISH SOUP WITH MILK [KALAKEITTO MAITOON]

Perch is the best fish for this soup; frozen perch gives a pretty good flavor. Fish tastes stronger in Finland; since in my American soup I need more fish for taste, the soup becomes almost stew-like.

2½ cups water
1½ teaspoons sea salt, or to taste
  3 whole allspice
  5 whole white peppercorns
  2 small onions, peeled and
     quartered
  1 lb potatoes, scraped and
     quartered

1–1½ lbs cleaned perch, fresh or
     frozen
1½ cups milk
  1 tablespoon unbleached white
     flour
  3 tablespoons chopped fresh dill
     leaves
  2 tablespoons chopped chives

Put the water, 1 teaspoon of the salt, the allspice, peppercorns, and onion quarters into a soup kettle. Cover, bring to a boil, and simmer 10 minutes. Add potatoes, cover, and simmer over a low heat 15 minutes.

Lower the heat to a minimum. Cut the fish into pieces and place them on top of the potatoes in the kettle. Sprinkle with the remaining ½ teaspoon salt. Cover and simmer 15 minutes, or until the fish is done.

Mix together the milk and flour so that there are no lumps. Pour it into the soup and stir gently. Turn the heat a little higher, cover partially, and simmer 10 minutes. Remove from the heat. Add the dill and chives. Cover the pot and let stand about 10 minutes before serving—to let the dill and chive tastes blend.

Serve hot with fresh bread as a whole-meal soup. Nothing more is needed.
Servings: 4 to 6.

SALMON SOUP [LOHIKEITTO]

This is a rich and tasty soup that's usually served as an appetizer before a light dinner. It's considered a true gourmet's delight.

  3 cups water or fish broth
  1 bay leaf
  1 leek, sliced into rings
  ¾ lb potatoes, peeled and cut into
     small cubes
  ¾ lb salmon (see Note)
  ¾ cup cream

1½ tablespoons unbleached white
     flour
  1 tablespoon butter
  1 teaspoon sea salt, or to taste
  ¼ teaspoon white pepper
     Pinch of allspice

Put the water, bay leaf, and leek into a soup kettle, cover, and bring to a boil. Simmer 10 minutes. Add potato cubes, cover, and simmer over a low heat 15 minutes, or until the potatoes are done.

Add the salmon, cut into cubes. Cover and simmer 5 minutes. Combine the cream and flour to make a smooth paste. Pour it slowly into the soup and stir. Cover only partially and simmer 5 minutes, or until the soup thickens. Add the butter. Remove from the heat, and add the salt, pepper, and allspice. Check the taste.

Serve hot as an appetizer soup. Little egg pastries (see page 168) are excellent with this soup.

Note: Salmon or lox trimmings—leftover pieces after the fish is cut into fillets and steaks—are great for making soup. If you use lox, omit the salt; lox is usually salty enough.

Servings: 4.

SMOKED SALMON SOUP [SYSMÄLÄINEN SAVULOHIKEITTO]

This soup originated in the village of Sysmä in Central Finland, by the legendary Lake Päijänne. An elegant appetizer soup, it combines the strong tastes of dill, smoke, and salmon.

4 cups water	¾–1 lb smoked salmon (see Note)
10 fresh dill stalks (reserve the leaves)	½ teaspoon coarse sea salt, or to taste
½ teaspoon dill seeds	2 tablespoons butter
¾ lb potatoes (preferably new), cubed	½ cup chopped fresh dill leaves
3 carrots, scraped and cubed	¼ teaspoon white pepper
1 leek, sliced into rings	Salt, if necessary

Put the water, dill stalks, and seeds into a soup kettle. Cover, bring to a boil, and simmer 15 minutes. Strain to remove the dill stalks and seeds. Add the potatoes, carrots, and leek to the broth. Cover and simmer over low heat 30 minutes, or until the vegetables are soft.

Add the smoked salmon, cut into cubes. Cover and simmer 5 minutes. Add the butter, chopped dill leaves, pepper, and salt. Turn off the heat. Cover and let sit at least 15 minutes to let the tastes blend. Reheat before serving.

Serve as an appetizer soup.

Note: In the original recipe the strong Finnish autumn dill is used to achieve the flavor. The seeds and the stalks give about the same result. Also, in Finland real smoked salmon—warm-smoked until done—is used. But if that's hard to get, use the smoked (Nova Scotia) lox which is readily available. When lox is used, less salt is needed.

Servings: 4.

Meat Soups

For these soups, use the dark meat of an older animal; it gives a stronger taste. Since meat soups improve when reheated, they can be made in large quantities, frozen, and quickly heated.

PEA SOUP [HERNEKEITTO]

Pea soup in Finland is Thursday food; it is school, army, and camp food, a great dish for community meals. It is served on Shrove Tuesday. The dessert after pea soup is traditionally the oven pancake.

2 cups dried green peas	1 carrot, scraped
4 cups water	1 teaspoon sea salt, or to taste
1 tablespoon sea salt	¼ teaspoon marjoram (optional)
5 cups water	1 tablespoon prepared mustard
1–1½ lbs smoked pork hocks	(optional)
1 onion, peeled and halved	

Soak the peas in 4 cups of salted water overnight. Strain the peas and discard the soaking water. Put the peas and 5 cups of water in a soup kettle. Bring to a boil, cover, and simmer over a low heat about 30 minutes.

Add the pork hocks, onion, and carrot. Simmer, covered, until the peas are soft and mushy, about 3 hours. If the water has been reduced, add more.

Take out the pork hocks, remove the skins, and cut the meat into little pieces. Put the meat back into the soup. Season with salt, if necessary. Add marjoram and mustard, if desired.

Another method: To make the soup more sophisticated, put it through a sieve and discard the pea shells. Add a couple of drops of Worcestershire sauce and some croutons. Serve the meat separately.

Pea soup is a satisfying whole-meal soup. It is even better when reheated. Make a large portion and freeze part of it.

Servings: 5 to 6.

BONE SOUP [LUUKEITTO]

Start this soup the day before. It doesn't require much work, for it will simmer happily by itself.

3 lbs marrow bones	1 large onion, quartered
5 cups water	5 tablespoons pearl barley
1 tablespoon sea salt, or to taste	Leftover cold meat (optional)
4 large potatoes, scraped and cubed	¼ teaspoon white pepper
2 carrots, scraped and sliced	⅛ teaspoon allspice
¼ medium-size rutabaga, peeled	¼ cup chopped parsley
and cubed	2 tablespoons lemon juice (optional)

Roast the bones in the broiler, about 10 minutes on each side.

Put the bones into a soup kettle and cover with cold water. Add salt. Bring to a boil very slowly, keeping the pot partially covered.

Cover and simmer over low heat 3 to 4 hours. Remove from the heat and let stand overnight in a cold place.

The next day, skim off the layer of fat from the surface. Remove the bones from the broth and reserve. Add the vegetables to the broth, cover, and simmer over a low heat 1 to 1½ hours, or until all vegetables are soft. Add the barley and any leftover cold meat, cubed. Cover and simmer about ½ hour, or until the barley is done.

Before serving, add pepper, allspice, parsley, and lemon juice, if desired. Check the taste. Heat the bones a little and serve them on a plate.

Serve with good bread as a whole-meal soup. Serve the bones for those who like them; the marrow is a great topping for bread.
Servings: 4.

TUESDAY SOUP [TIISTAIKEITTO]

If ham was served on Sunday, the cold leftovers were eaten on Monday and the bone was made into a soup on Tuesday. Add some smoked pork hocks and you will have a great mellow soup.

Leftover ham bones	*6–8 small red potatoes, unpeeled,*
1 lb smoked pork hocks	*quartered*
4 cups water	*¼ teaspoon celery seed*
1 tablespoon sea salt, or to taste	*Leftover ham, sausage, or meat*
1/3 cup pearl barley	*pieces (optional)*
Juice from a pork roast (optional)	*1 cup milk*
¼ medium-size rutabaga, peeled and	*1 tablespoon unbleached white flour*
cut into strips	*¼ teaspoon white pepper*
2 carrots, sliced	*¼ cup chopped parsley*
½ parsnip, peeled and sliced	

Put the ham bones and pork hocks into a soup kettle. Cover with cold water, add salt, and bring to a boil. Lower the heat, cover, and simmer 1½ to 2 hours. Rinse the barley and add it to the soup. Add any juice from a pork roast you may have. Throw in the rutabaga, carrots, parsnip, potatoes, and celery seed. Cover and simmer ½ hour.

Remove the ham bone and pork hocks. Remove the skin from the hocks and cut the meat into small pieces. Put the meat back into the kettle. Add any other leftover meat you have.

Make a smooth paste of the milk and flour. Pour it into the soup, stirring. Simmer 10 minutes. Add the pepper and parsley. Check the taste.

Serve as a main course. Serve with good bread and possibly some cheese.
Servings: 4.

MEAT SOUP [LIHASOPPA]

½ medium rutabaga, peeled and
   cubed
3 carrots, scraped and sliced
1 small parsnip, peeled and sliced
½ celery root, peeled and cubed, or
   ½ teaspoon celery seed
1 leek, sliced
1 onion, peeled and quartered
1½ lbs bony beef (shank, breast, or
   shoulder)

5 cups water
2 teaspoons sea salt, or to taste
6–10 potatoes, scraped and quartered
¼ cup chopped parsley
¼ teaspoon white pepper
⅛ teaspoon allspice
2 tablespoons lemon juice
   (optional)

Roast the vegetables (except the potatoes) in a heavy frying pan without fat, until they are lightly browned. Combine them with the meat in a heavy soup kettle. Cover with cold water and add salt. Bring to a boil slowly and simmer, covered, over low heat 1 to 1½ hours.

Add the potatoes, cover, and simmer 1 more hour. Before serving, remove the meat and cut it into little pieces. Discard the bones, and put the meat pieces back into the soup. Add chopped parsley, pepper, allspice, and lemon juice, if desired. Check the salt.

Serve with fresh bread as a whole-meal soup.
Servings: 4 to 6.

LAMB AND VEGETABLE SOUP [LAMMAS-JUURESKEITTO]

1 tablespoon butter
1–1½ lbs bony lamb breast, shank, or
   shoulder
1 tablespoon unbleached white
   flour
5 cups water or broth made from
   a leftover lamb bone
1 onion, quartered
2 carrots, scraped and sliced
1 small parsnip, peeled, and sliced
4–6 Jerusalem (root) artichokes,
   peeled and cubed (optional)

½ small cauliflower, cut into
   flowerettes
¼ teaspoon celery seed, or a piece
   of celery root
1 tablespoon sea salt
1 cup fresh or frozen peas
¼ teaspoon white pepper
¼ cup chopped parsley
2 tablespoons lemon juice
   (optional)

Brown the butter in a large kettle. Cut the bony meat into a few pieces and brown it on all sides. Sprinkle the meat with the flour and brown it. Heat the water or broth and pour it over the meat.

Add the onion, carrots, parsnip, artichokes, cauliflower, celery seed, and salt. Cover and simmer over a low heat for 2 hours.

Remove the bony meat, cut off the meat, and return the meat to the kettle. Add the peas, cover, and simmer 10 minutes.

Before serving, add pepper, parsley, and lemon juice, if desired. Serve with bread as a whole meal.
Servings: 4 to 6.

SAUERKRAUT SOUP [HAPANKAALI]

Influenced by the Russian sauerkraut soup, this dish is popular in winter. Make it either from homemade sauerkraut (see page 120) or the commercial variety.

1 lb smoked pork hocks (2 medium pieces)	½ teaspoon raw sugar or honey
4 cups water	⅛ teaspoon white pepper
2½ cups sauerkraut	1 teaspoon mustard
2 tablespoons unbleached pastry flour	1 tablespoon tomato puree (optional)
¼ cup cold water	5–6 good frankfurters, cut into 1-inch pieces

Put the pork hocks into cold water, heat, and simmer 1 to 1½ hours. Add the sauerkraut, cover, and simmer over a very low heat 1 to 1½ hours. Remove the hocks, take the skin off, and cut the meat into small pieces. Put them back into the soup.

Mix the flour and water into a smooth paste. Pour the paste slowly into the soup and stir. Simmer 5 minutes. Add the sugar, white pepper, mustard, and tomato puree, if used. Add the frankfurter pieces, cover, and simmer 5 minutes. Check the salt, and add if necessary.

Serve as a main course. Add a spoonful of sour cream to your serving, if you wish.

Servings: 4 to 6.

CABBAGE SOUP [KAALIKEITTO]

½–¾ lb bony lamb (breast, shank, or neck)	2 tablespoons butter
½ lb bony beef	1 tablespoon white vinegar
½ lb bony pork	½ teaspoon marjoram leaves, ground
3–5 cups water (see Note)	1 teaspoon raw sugar or honey (optional)
1 tablespoon sea salt, or to taste	
2 lbs cabbage	

Put all of the meat into a heavy soup kettle. Cover with cold water, add salt, and bring to a boil. Lower the heat, cover, and simmer 2 to 3 hours.

Discard the outer cabbage leaves, and chop the cabbage coarsely. Heat a large, heavy frying pan and add the butter. (You may need 2 frying pans for this amount of cabbage.) The pan should not be too hot. Fry the cabbage slowly, about 20 minutes, stirring every now and then. "Scare" the cabbage by pouring the vinegar over it. This will eliminate some of the odor. Put the cabbage into the soup kettle.

Cover the kettle. Simmer over a low heat 1 to 1½ hours. Add marjoram and sugar, if desired. Remove the meat, cut it off the bones, and put the meat pieces back into the kettle. Check the taste.

Another method: At the same time as you add the cabbage, it is possible to add 4 to 6 quartered potatoes. You may also add ⅛ teaspoon allspice. The cabbage may be added into the soup unfried—in that case, increase its cooking time to 2 or 2½ hours.

Serve as a main course, with sour rye bread.

Note: The amount of water will vary depending upon whether the cabbage is new or old. The bright green heads of new cabbage yield more water. If you use new cabbage, be careful not to let the soup become too watery. At first use only 3 cups of water; after simmering the soup with the cabbage, check the water and add more if necessary

Servings: 4 to 6.

KIDNEY SOUP [MUNUAISKEITTO]

This recipe dates back to 1901 and is probably of German origin. It is an inexpensive and interesting soup for those who like kidneys.

1½ lbs veal or beef kidneys
4 cups water
1½ teaspoons sea salt, or to taste
1 carrot, diced
¼ small rutabaga, diced
½ parsnip, diced
½ leek, sliced
1 piece celery root, or ¼ teaspoon celery seed

1 small red onion, chopped
¼ teaspoon ginger
1½ tablespoons unbleached white flour
¼ cup cold water
3 tablespoons lemon juice
½ teaspoon raw sugar or honey
Dash of cayenne

Clean the kidneys, remove all of the fat, and cut into small pieces. Put them into a soup kettle together with the salt and water. Bring to a boil, cover, and simmer about 15 minutes.

Meanwhile, roast all of the vegetables plus the celery seed, if used, in a heavy, ungreased frying pan until light brown. Put the vegetables into the kettle. Add the ginger. Cover and simmer over a low heat until the kidneys and vegetables are soft, about 1 hour.

Mix the water and flour together into a smooth paste, and pour it into the soup, stirring well. Simmer until the soup thickens. Season with lemon juice, sugar or honey, and cayenne.

Serve hot as a main course.
Servings: 4 to 6.

Vegetable Soups

The vegetable soups are either light appetizer soups or hearty enough to be served as the main course. With such soups, open-face sandwiches are often served.

VEGETABLE BROTH [VIHANNESLIEMI]

It is difficult to give exact amounts of the vegetables since the combination can vary. Use several or all of the listed vegetables and make your own kind of broth.

½ cauliflower, cut into flowerettes
1 cup Brussels sprouts
4–6 Jerusalem (root) artichokes, halved
1 carrot, scraped and sliced
1 turnip, peeled and cubed
1 cup peas, with pods

1 small parsnip, peeled and sliced
1 onion, peeled and quartered
2 small leeks, sliced
4–6 stalks parsley
5–6 cups water
1½ teaspoons sea salt, or to taste

Put all of the vegetables and parsley into a soup kettle. Pour cold water over them and add salt. Bring to a boil, lower the heat, cover, and simmer very slowly about 2 hours.

Strain the broth and discard the vegetables. Use the clear broth either plain or as a base for other soups.

As an appetizer, serve with parsley and dill. Or thicken the broth with an egg. Or you may add a few whole, cooked vegetables—Brussels sprouts, scallion rings, or julienne carrots—to the broth.

Servings: 4 to 6.

PEA POD SOUP [HERNEENPALKOKEITTO]

A clever use of leftovers—a soup dating from the turn of the century.

1 lb pea pods, empty
5 cups mild broth (vegetable, beef, or chicken)
1½ tablespoons unbleached white flour
¼ cup water

1 tablespoon finely chopped fresh dill, or 1 teaspoon dried dill
1 tablespoon chopped fresh parsley, or 1 teaspoon dried parsley
1 teaspoon butter (optional)

Use the peas from the pods for another purpose. Remove the tips and strings from the pods. Bring the broth to a boil, put the pods in the kettle, cover, and simmer over a very low heat until the pods are soft, about 20 minutes.

Pour the soup through a sieve. Rub the pods against it, so that everything but the hard parts goes through. Discard the pulp. Heat the soup. Mix the flour and water into a smooth paste, and pour it into the soup. Simmer about 5 minutes. Add the dill, parsley, and butter, if desired. Check the salt, add some if necessary.

Serve as an appetizer.
Servings: 4 to 5.

DILL SOUP [TILLIKEITTO]

4 cups water
½ teaspoon sea salt, or to taste
¾ lb potatoes, peeled and cubed
2 carrots, scraped and cubed

1 cup chopped fresh dill leaves
⅛ teaspoon white pepper, or to taste
2 tablespoons cream (optional)

Bring the salted water to a boil and add the potatoes and carrots. Cover and simmer over a low heat about ½ hour, or until the vegetables are soft.

Put through a sieve or blend in a blender. Add the dill and reheat. Add pepper and cream, if desired.

Serve as an appetizer, either hot or chilled. The color must be truly green, and the dill must taste strong.
Servings: 4.

SUMMER SOUP [KESÄKEITTO]

Ideally, young, sweet, fresh vegetables should be used. In Finland this is a seasonal dish, made of the very first tender vegetables of the summer. A frozen mix for the soup is sold nowadays.

1 small cauliflower, cut into
   flowerettes
2–3 young carrots, sliced
6–8 small new potatoes, quartered
1 onion, quartered
1 cup green peas, fresh or frozen
¼ cup sugar peas (optional)
¼ cup string beans, cut into pieces
1½ cups water, or to barely cover the
   vegetables

3 cups milk
1½ tablespoons unbleached white
   flour
¼ cup (½ stick) butter
1 teaspoon sea salt, or to taste
½ teaspoon raw sugar (optional; if
   the vegetables aren't very young,
   this gives the sweetness)
⅛ teaspoon white pepper
1/3 cup chopped fresh parsley

Put all the vegetables into a soup kettle. Cover with water, bring to a boil, cover, and simmer over low heat until the vegetables are done, about ½ hour.

Add all but 1/3 cup of the milk. With the remainder of the milk and the flour, make a smooth paste, and stir it into the soup. Cover the pot partially, and simmer about 10 minutes.

Remove from heat, add the butter, salt, sugar if used, pepper, and parsley. Cover, and let stand 5 minutes.

Serve as a main course, with fresh bread or with cheese sandwiches. This soup is very good when reheated. When you reheat, do not let it boil.
Servings: 6 to 8.

NETTLE SOUP [NOKKOSKEITTO]

Nettles have even more vitamins and iron than spinach. Pick young, tender nettle leaves. Pick them in the spring, and dry or freeze them as you would spinach.

6 cups small, young nettle leaves
4 cups broth (vegetable, chicken, or
    beef)
1 cup milk
1½ tablespoons unbleached white
    flour
¼ cup cold water
¼ teaspoon sea salt, or to taste
⅛ teaspoon raw sugar or honey
⅛ teaspoon white pepper
2 tablespoons chopped chives
½ teaspoon crushed chervil
    (optional)
1 tablespoon butter (optional)

Rinse the nettles and put them into a saucepan. Steam them, using only the rinsing water, until limp. Chop.

In a saucepan, combine the broth and milk. Heat and bring to a boil. Mix the flour and cold water into a smooth paste and add it to the liquid, stirring well. Simmer about 10 minutes, or until the soup thickens.

Add the chopped nettles and simmer 5 minutes. Remove from the heat and add salt, sugar or honey, pepper, chives, chervil, and butter, if desired. Cover and let stand 10 minutes. Before serving, reheat carefully, if necessary, but do not let boil.

Serve as an appetizer or as a light main course. Some people like to put hard-boiled egg halves into the soup. It looks decorative and adds protein to the meal.
Servings: 4 to 6.

CARROT SOUP [PORKKANAKEITTO]

4 cups beef or vegetable broth
½ lb young carrots, sliced
¼ celery root, or ¼ teaspoon
    celery seed
1 leek, cut into rings
½ parsnip, peeled and cut into slices

1 tablespoon butter
1 tablespoon unbleached white flour
½ teaspoon sea salt, or to taste
⅛ teaspoon white pepper, or to taste
¼ cup cream
¼ cup finely chopped parsley

Bring the broth to a boil, and add the vegetables. Cover, and simmer until the vegetables are done, about ½ hour. Put the mixture through a sieve, or blend in blender.

Melt the butter in the kettle, add flour, and cook about 3 minutes. Do not let brown. Add the pureed vegetable mix little by little, letting the mixture simmer after each addition.

Simmer 5 minutes. Add salt and pepper.

Remove from heat, and add cream and parsley.

Serve hot, as an appetizer or as a light main course with sandwiches.
Servings: 4.

MUSHROOM SOUP [SIENIKEITTO]

3 cups cleaned, sliced mushrooms
2 tablespoons butter
1½ tablespoons unbleached white
    flour
4 cups veal or chicken broth
2 tablespoons sour cream

1 tablespoon lemon juice
1 egg yolk (optional)
½ teaspoon sea salt, or to taste
⅛ teaspoon white pepper, or to
    taste

Put the sliced mushrooms and butter into a saucepan. Cover with a tight lid, and cook about 15 minutes, or until the mushrooms are soft and limp.

Sprinkle the mushrooms with flour, stir, and let the flour become golden, but not brown. Warm the broth. Pour the broth slowly, a little at a time over the mushrooms, stirring constantly, and letting thicken after each addition. Lower the heat, cover the saucepan, and simmer the soup slowly about 30 minutes.

Beat together the sour cream and lemon juice. Remove the soup from heat, and stir the sour cream mixture in. If the egg yolk is used—it's really not necessary, for the soup is rich enough—beat it lightly, add ¼ cup hot broth to it, and stir into the soup. Season with salt and pepper.

Serve in a small cup as an appetizer. The soup is satisfying enough to be had also as a main course, with hot or cold open-face sandwiches.
Servings: 4 to 6.

OLD KARELIAN MUSHROOM-BARLEY SOUP
[KARJALAINEN TATTIKEITTO]

The strong-flavored wild mushrooms were used for this soup, which is one of the very old dishes in this book. It has a true home-cooked taste and gives a warm feeling. Try making it with black mushrooms.

1/3 cup barley (preferably hulled)
3 cups water, mild broth, or liquid
    from boiling vegetables
1 teaspoon sea salt, or to taste

½ lb mushrooms, sliced
1½ cups milk, or a mixture of light
    cream and milk
1 tablespoon butter

Rinse barley, and soak it in the liquid a few hours, or overnight. Put it into a soup kettle, add salt, and bring to a boil. Cover, and simmer over low heat until the barley is done.

Add the mushrooms, milk and butter. Cover partially, and simmer 15 minutes. Check salt.

Serve hot, as an appetizer, or even as a whole-meal soup, with sandwiches.
Servings: 4 to 5.

MILK AND CABBAGE SOUP [MAITOKAALI]

This soup has a mild and milky taste, quite different from what you would expect from a cabbage dish. Children like it. Tender, young new cabbage gives the best taste.

3 cups milk	¼ cup cold water
1½ cups water	1 tablespoon unbleached white flour
⅛ teaspoon white pepper, or to taste	½ teaspoon sea salt, or to taste
⅛ teaspoon allspice	¼ teaspoon raw sugar
1 bay leaf	1 tablespoon butter (optional)
5 cups chopped young, green cabbage	

In a heavy-bottomed saucepan or in the top of a double boiler, combine the milk and water. Add the white pepper, allspice, and bay leaf. Heat and bring to a boil. Add the chopped cabbage. Lower the heat, cover the pot partially, and let simmer slowly until the cabbage is soft. Young cabbage should cook in ½ hour.

Combine the cold water and flour to make a smooth paste. Pour it into the soup, stir, and let simmer about 10 minutes, or until the soup thickens a little. Remove the bay leaf; after removing the soup from the heat, season with salt and sugar. A lump of butter adds to the taste.

Serve as an appetizer or as a light lunch or dinner soup.
Servings: 4 to 6.

Chapter 5

CASSEROLES AND POTS
[LAATIKOT JA PADAT]

Oven-cooked casseroles and pot dishes are typical Finnish food, and they still are as popular as ever: many of the traditional ones are now being produced commercially. They are great for everyday cooking; they are always inexpensive, and quick to combine. I have included both traditional dishes and some new variations.

Casseroles

Casseroles are made of layers of meat, fish and vegetables—often potatoes—and baked in a shallow, uncovered oven dish. A typical casserole requires a mixture of milk and eggs that is poured over the ingredients. Casseroles are cooked faster than pots, and they usually require a higher temperature.

Shallow glass or earthenware dishes are best for making casseroles. Glass cake pans and loaf pans are good for most dishes.

SMELT AND BACON CASSEROLE [SILAKKALAATIKKO]

The taste combination of smelts, bacon, and potatoes is good, in a basic sort of way. In Finland this dish is part of the regular family menu. It appears also on restaurant lunch lists, for those who favor home cooking.

1 tablespoon butter	1 onion, peeled and sliced thinly
1½ lbs potatoes, peeled and sliced thinly	6 thick strips bacon, cut into 1-inch pieces
½ lb cleaned, butterflied small smelts	1 egg
1½ teaspoons sea salt	1½ cups milk
¼ teaspoon white pepper	

Preheat the oven to 400°F. With half the butter, grease well an ovenproof glass dish. Combine the casserole: first a layer of potato slices, then a layer of smelts sprinkled with salt and pepper, a layer of onion slices, and a layer of bacon. Repeat if necessary. The top layer will be potatoes sprinkled with salt, pepper, and bacon.

Beat the egg lightly, add milk, and beat. Pour over the casserole. Dot with the rest of the butter. Bake about 1 hour, or until there is a dark brown, crisp crust— the best part of the dish!—on the top and sides.

Serve for lunch or dinner. Accompany with pickled beets (see page 117) or hatched beets (see page 113). Some people like to sprinkle water-diluted vinegar over the dish.
Servings: 4 to 5.

SMELTS IN TOMATO SAUCE [TOMAATTISILAKAT]

An easy and quick casserole. The tomato sauce brings out the slightly sweet flavor of the smelts in an interesting way.

½–¾ lb cleaned small smelts	¼ cup tomato puree
1 can anchovies, preferably Scandinavian	½ cup cream
⅛ teaspoon white pepper	1 teaspoon butter or oil
	2 tablespoons chopped parsley

Preheat the oven to 400°F. Remove the backbones from the smelts. Inside each fish, place one anchovy or a piece of anchovy, depending on their saltiness. Grease a shallow flameproof dish, and place the fish in it, tightly side by side. Sprinkle with pepper.

Mix together the tomato puree and cream, and spoon it over the fish. Dot lightly with butter or sprinkle with oil. Bake about 20 minutes. The surface of the dish should dry a little, and be brown. Sprinkle with parsley.

Serve as a lunch or dinner dish, with potatoes and/or bread, and a light green salad.
Servings: 4.

SMOKED FISH CASSEROLE [SAVUKALALAATIKKO]

This is most often made of raw and smoked Baltic Herring. For best results use some fish that you can buy both raw and smoked; but if not available, use any kind of fish.

1 tablespoon butter	*3 tablespoons chopped fresh dill, or*
½ lb cleaned fish fillets	*1 teaspoon dried*
½ lb smoked fish	*¾ cup light cream*
½ teaspoon sea salt	*4 tablespoons shredded Swiss cheese*
¼ teaspoon white pepper, or to taste	*2 tablespoons bread crumbs*

Preheat the oven to 400°F. Butter a shallow oven casserole. Cut the fish—both raw and smoked—into 1-inch pieces.

Start with a layer of raw fish, sprinkle it with salt, pepper, and dill. Top it with a layer of smoked fish. Repeat. Pour the cream over the casserole, sprinkle with cheese and bread crumbs. Bake ½ hour, or until the surface is crisp and brown.

Serve as a lunch, dinner, or after-sauna dish.
Servings: 4.

FISH CASSEROLE [KALAPAISTOS]

1 onion, chopped	*2 tablespoons chopped parsley*
1 tablespoon butter or oil	*1 tablespoon capers*
2 cups flaked leftover boiled or fried	*2 tablespoons lemon juice*
fish	*¼ teaspoon sea salt, or to taste*
4 tablespoons bread crumbs	*¼ teaspoon white pepper*
4 tablespoons shredded Swiss cheese	*2 eggs, beaten*

Preheat the oven to 400°F. Fry the onion in half of the oil or butter and cool slightly. Mix together the onion, flaked fish, bread crumbs, cheese, parsley, capers, lemon juice, salt, and pepper. Beat the eggs, and stir into the mixture.

Grease a shallow oven dish with the rest of the oil or butter, and pour in the mixture. Bake 20 to 30 minutes.

Serve for lunch with a grated salad (see page 115).
Servings: 4.

SALMON CASSEROLE [LOHILAATIKKO]

If you are going to have a buffet or smorgasbord, this is a great hot dish to serve. It is one of the best casseroles I know of.

1 tablespoon butter	½ teaspoon sea salt, or to taste
3–4 tablespoons bread crumbs	3 eggs
1½ lbs potatoes, peeled and sliced thin	1½ cups cream
½–¾ lb lox or salmon trimmings (see Note), or 1 large can salmon	1 teaspoon raw sugar or honey

Preheat the oven to 400°F. Use half of the butter to grease a 2-quart ovenproof dish. Sprinkle heavily with half of the bread crumbs.

To combine the casserole, first arrange a layer of potato slices, then a layer of salmon pieces. Repeat as many times as necessary. Sprinkle the potatoes lightly with salt. The top layer will be potatoes.

Beat the eggs lightly, add cream, sugar or honey, and salt. Beat. Pour over the casserole. Sprinkle the top with the rest of the bread crumbs, and dot with the rest of the butter.

Bake about 1 hour, or until the top and sides have a nice brown, crisp crust.

This is an elegant lunch or dinner dish, or a good warm dish for a buffet table. Serve with a little vinegar diluted with water, and/or melted butter. Some colorful, light salad—grated carrots (see page 115), pickled beets (see page 117), or a green salad with lemon—is all you need to accompany it.

Note: Some stores sell lox trimmings, which are marvelously economical for soups and casseroles.

Servings: 4 to 6.

JANSSON'S TEMPTATION [JANSSONIN KIUSAUS]

This Scandinavian dish is known as a late party snack, when people get a craving for something salty.

8 medium-size potatoes	Liquid from the anchovies
2 onions, sliced thin	1½ cups cream
16 anchovy fillets (preferably Scandinavian)	2 tablespoons butter

Preheat the oven to 400°F. Peel the raw potatoes and cut into julienne strips. Rinse them with cold running water, and drain well on paper towels.

Butter a shallow oven casserole. Combine layers of potatoes, onions, and anchovies. The top layer will be potatoes. Mix together the cream and the anchovy juice, and pour over the casserole. Dot with the rest of the butter. Bake about 45 minutes, or until the liquid is almost absorbed, the potatoes are soft, and the surface brown.

Serve as a late party dish, or for lunch or dinner.

Servings: 6 to 8.

OLD FINNISH MUSHROOM-CABBAGE CASSEROLE
[VANHA SUOMALAINEN SIENI-KAALILAATIKKO]

This is a light and rather mellow dish, good for a change after spicy foods and heavy meat dishes.

1/3 cup pearl barley, or whole barley
1½ cups milk
    4 cups cabbage, shredded
    1 cup carrots, grated
    2 cups mushrooms, sliced

1 egg, lightly beaten
1 teaspoon sea salt
¼ teaspoon white pepper
1 tablespoon butter or oil
2 tablespoons bread crumbs

Soak the barley in milk 4 to 5 hours, or overnight. Preheat the oven to 400°F. Mix all the vegetables together, and add the milk-barley mixture. Add the lightly beaten egg, salt, and pepper. Mix well.

Grease a 2-quart ovenproof dish, and pour the mixture in. Press down. Sprinkle the top with bread crumbs. Bake 1½ hours.

Another method: You may also fry the cabbage and the mushrooms before mixing all the vegetables together. The dish will have a stronger taste, and it will also be heavier. Fry the cabbage slowly, about ½ hour, until it's brown. Fry the mushrooms quickly, about 5 minutes, until brown. Cool a little before combining.

Serve as a lunch or dinner main dish, with lingonberry jam. Or use to accompany a meat dish.
Servings: 4 to 6.

CABBAGE CASSEROLE [KAALILAATIKKO]

This is one of the Finnish classics, known in schools as well as in homes, and loved by many. It is a strong-tasting dish, if made correctly.

2 tablespoons oil
1 tablespoon butter
1 large head of winter cabbage,
  shredded coarsely

1 lb ground meat
1 teaspoon sea salt

In a heavy frying pan, heat the mixture of oil and butter, and when it's brown, add the cabbage, which should be browned slowly as if to persuade the taste to come out. The heat should not be high. The browning will take half an hour. The cabbage will become brown and rather limp. Remove the cabbage with a slotted spoon, draining off some of the fat.

Brown the meat quickly in the same pan. Remove. Use some of the pan fat to grease a 2-quart oven casserole. Preheat the oven to 350°F. Combine the cabbage, meat, and salt. Pour it into the casserole, and press down. Bake 1 to 1½ hours, or until the top has browned.

Lingonberry jam is a must with this dish—it needs nothing else. Serve as a dinner dish. Cabbage casserole is always better when reheated. That makes it a popular ready-made dish.
Servings: 4 to 6.

OLD-FASHIONED LIVER CASSEROLE
[VANHAN AJAN MAKSALAATIKKO]

This dish is rather exotic, with the sweetness of raisins and the aroma of the liver and herbs. It's a very old Western Finland dish, but still popular, and sold in stores as a ready-made dish. It's pure health food and worth trying.

2 cups water	1 teaspoon sea salt
1 cup milk	½ teaspoon white pepper
1 cup pearl barley or brown rice	1 teaspoon marjoram leaves,
1 large onion, chopped	crushed
1 tablespoon vegetable oil	⅛ teaspoon ginger (optional)
¾ lb ground liver (see Note)	1/3 cup seedless raisins
¼ cup corn syrup or blackstrap	1 egg, beaten lightly
molasses (see Note)	1 teaspoon oil for the casserole

In a saucepan, combine the water and milk. Bring to a boil and add the barley. Simmer 10 minutes, stirring once in a while. Cover, and let hatch (see page 3) until all the liquid is absorbed. Cool.

Preheat the oven to 350°F. Fry the chopped onion in oil until soft and light brown. Cool slightly. In a large mixing bowl, combine the barley porridge, onion, ground liver, corn syrup or molasses, salt, pepper, marjoram, ginger, raisins, and egg. Mix well.

Oil a 3-quart ovenproof casserole. Pour the liver mixture in and bake about 1 hour. The top should be browned, but not burned.

Serve with melted butter and lingonberry or cranberry preserves.

Note: Ask your butcher to put the liver through a meat grinder. The liver will be quite soupy, so don't panic. It is possible to grind the liver at home in a meat grinder.

Corn syrup is closer in taste to the Finnish syrup, but if you want to make this dish a health bomb, use iron-rich blackstrap molasses.

Servings: 6 to 8.

MUSHROOM CASSEROLE [SIENILAATIKKO]

This is seemingly simple, but turns out so tasty and mellow. It's a meal in itself, and you don't even miss your meat.

Mashed potatoes:

1 lb potatoes	¼ teaspoon white pepper
1 cup milk	⅛ teaspoon mace (optional)
½ teaspoon sea salt	1 egg yolk (optional)

Mushroom mixture:

1 lb mushrooms, chopped	1 teaspoon sea salt, or to taste
1 onion, chopped	
2 tablespoons butter or oil	1 teaspoon butter or oil
	3 tablespoons bread crumbs

Boil the potatoes in their jackets until done. While still hot, peel the potatoes and mash them. Heat the milk and add it to the potatoes a little at a time. Mix well. Beat well until light and airy. Add salt and pepper, and if used, mace and egg yolk.

Mix the onion and mushrooms. Heat the butter or oil in a heavy frying pan. The pan should be hot enough so that the mushrooms brown quickly. You know it's hot enough if the liquid from the mushrooms evaporates immediately and does not stay in the pan. Stir well while frying. When brown, remove from the pan, and season with salt.

Preheat the oven to 350°F. Grease a 2-quart oven casserole, and sprinkle it heavily with half of the bread crumbs. Combine the casserole: first a layer of mashed potatoes, then a layer of mushrooms. Repeat. The top will be mashed potatoes. Press down slightly. Sprinkle with the rest of the bread crumbs, and dot with the rest of butter or sprinkle with the oil. Bake about 1 hour, or until the top and the sides have a nice crispy coating.

Serve as a main dish with cucumber salad, lingonberry jam and bread. Or use to accompany a meat or fish dish, in which case this recipe will serve more people.
Servings: 4 to 6.

Pots

Pots are made in deep dishes with lids. "Hatching" is used to prepare pot dishes. It started in the old days, when the houses were heated by wood, and the cold Finnish climate made it necessary to prepare food on the same low, continuous fire that heated the house. Often hatching was done in the afterheat—the mild heat that stays in the oven after the cooking that requires high heat is completed.

Now hatching is used simply to bring out the hidden strength of flavors. It is gentle to vitamins as well as tastes. The best hatching is done slowly, below the actual boiling point. The ingredients should be treated gently even before being put into the pot; if the meat has to be browned, do not shock it with hot, angry heat.

Not too much liquid should be used, because the lid is kept tight on the pot, and hardly any liquid evaporates. The steam that forms inside the pot will cook it.

Glass pots with a lid are great for this; they distribute heat evenly, and allow one to watch how the cooking is going. Clay and terracotta pots, cast-iron kettles, and Dutch ovens are also good for hatching.

PERCH STEW [AHVENMUHENNOS]

4 perch fillets, fresh or frozen
1½ teaspoons sea salt, or to taste
1 tablespoon butter
1/3 cup chopped fresh parsley
1/3 cup chopped fresh dill leaves
¼ cup chopped fresh chives

2 tablespoons unbleached white
flour
2/3 cup water or fish broth (cooked
from the head and bones of the
fish, if you have saved them)

Rub the perch fillets with salt. Set aside. Grease a shallow ovenproof dish with half of the butter. Make a green bed of a mixture of parsley, dill, and chives. Use about half of the herbs. Lay the fish fillets side by side on the bed. Cover them with the rest of the herb mixture. Dot with the rest of the butter.

Preheat the oven to 300°F. In a saucepan, mix until smooth the flour and water or broth. Heat and bring to a boil, stirring well. Simmer about 5 minutes, or until the mixture thickens. Pour it over the perch. Cover the casserole with lid or foil. Hatch 30 to 40 minutes, or until the fish is done—soft and juicy.

Another method: Instead of perch, try some other strong-tasting fish.

Serve with boiled potatoes and a tart, colorful salad.
Servings: 4.

FISH AND VEGETABLE POT [KALA-VIHANNESPATA]

This recipe is a fairly recent one, but it still follows the traditional Finnish way of cooking.

1 tablespoon butter
1 tablespoon oil
2 leeks, cut into 2-inch pieces
4 ripe tomatoes, cut into wedges
3 carrots, scraped and sliced
1 lb cleaned pike, cut into steaks
1 lb cleaned whiting, cut into pieces
2 teaspoons sea salt, or to taste

½ cup peas, fresh or frozen
1/3 cup chopped fresh dill leaves
¼ cup chopped fresh parsley
¼ cup chopped fresh chives
Pinch of chervil
⅛ teaspoon white pepper
Juice of 1 lemon

Preheat the oven to 300°F. Combine the oil and butter in a frying pan, and fry the leeks, carrots, and tomatoes quickly.

Put the fish pieces into an ovenproof dish with a lid. Sprinkle with salt. Pour the vegetables from the frying pan over them. Add the peas. Sprinkle with dill, parsley, chives, and chervil. Dust with white pepper and pour the lemon juice over.

Cover, and bake 30 to 40 minutes, or until everything is done.

Serve on a bed of rice.
Servings: 4 to 6.

PORK AND SMALL TURNIP POT
[SIANLIHAA JA PIENIÄ NAURIITA]

2½ lbs lean pork butt, cut into 1-inch
   cubes
 1 tablespoon butter
10 tiny white turnips, or 5 medium
   ones, peeled and quartered
 2 tablespoons unbleached white
   flour
1½ cups beef broth
 ½ teaspoon raw sugar or honey
 ½ teaspoon sea salt, or to taste
 ¼ teaspoon white pepper, or to
   taste
   Pinch of thyme
 1 parsley sprig

Brown the pork cubes in half of the butter. Remove, and put them into a flame-proof deep casserole or a pot with a lid. Preheat the oven to 350°F.

Brown the turnips in the rest of the butter. Sprinkle with flour, turn, and let brown but not burn. Pour the beef broth over the turnips, a small amount at a time, stirring and letting it simmer after each addition. Simmer until the sauce thickens. Add sugar or honey, salt, pepper, and thyme. Stir.

Pour the turnip mixture over the pork in the pot. Mix, and add the sprig of parsley. Cover, and put the pot into the oven for 20 minutes. Lower the heat to 200°F. Hatch until the pork and turnips are soft, 1½ to 2 hours. Do not let the turnips become overdone.

Serve for dinner with potatoes and/or bread to dip into the juice, and some tart pickle or salad. Beer accompanies this dish best.
Servings: 4 to 6.

KARELIAN POT [KARJALANPAISTI]

This old dish has kept its popularity to the present day, and is now sold in cans. The long hatching brings out and combines the meat flavors, and no extra seasoning is necessary.

1 lb lean, boneless stewing pork
1 lb lean, boneless stewing beef
1 lb lean, boneless stewing lamb
1 tablespoon sea salt, or to taste

1 teaspoon whole white peppercorns
   (optional)
1 cup water (there will be juice and
   fat that come from the meats)

Preheat the oven to 300°F. Put all the meats, cut into 1-inch cubes, into a deep, ovenproof pot with a lid. Sprinkle with salt and with pepper, if used, and add the water. Cover, and let hatch 3 to 5 hours. If the pot simmers too quickly, lower the heat. Check the salt.

Serve for dinner with potatoes, and bread to dip. Add lingonberry preserves or a tart salad. This dish freezes well, and is even better when reheated.
Servings: 6 to 8.

PORK AND CABBAGE POT [SIANLIHA-KAALIPATA]

You start this 2 days before serving: it is not much trouble and the taste is certainly worth the planning ahead. This dish is from Countess Eva Mannerheim-Sparre's cookbook.

1 lb firm, white cabbage, chopped coarsely	¼ teaspoon ground white pepper, or to taste
1 teaspoon coarse sea salt	¼ cup white wine
1½ lbs pork tenderloin	

Mix the chopped cabbage with salt in a ceramic bowl, and let stand at room temperature 1 day.

The next day, cut the pork tenderloin into slices. Preheat the oven to 400°F. Put the cabbage and pork into an ovenproof dish with a lid. Sprinkle with pepper and pour the wine over. Mix, cover, and simmer in the oven for 20 minutes.

Lower the heat to 225°F. Hatch 1 hour. Take out of the oven and let cool. Keep until the next day.

Now the dish is finally ready to be served. Preheat the oven to 200°F. Put the pot into the oven and heat slowly until hot.

Serve with bread and lingonberry or cranberry preserves.
Servings: 4.

OLD KARELIAN PORK POT [PIRONA]

This old recipe provides strong nourishment—real winter food. A large portion was always made, to use the leftovers as cold cuts.

½ cup dry green peas	1 white turnip, cubed
½ cup beans or lentils (see Note)	½ medium rutabaga, cubed
5 cups water	4 potatoes, cubed
1½ teaspoons sea salt, or to taste	½ cup barley (pearl, hulled, or whole)
1½ lbs boneless pork butt or shoulder	

Soak the peas and beans overnight. Drain, discard the soaking water. Put the peas, beans, water, and salt into an iron pot, or some other heavy dish that can be used in the oven as well. Cover and simmer until soft, 1½ to 2 hours.

Preheat the oven to 350°F. Add the cubed pork, turnip, rutabaga, and potatoes. Stir in barley. Cover and bake ½ hour. Lower the heat to 225°F, and hatch 1½ to 2 hours, or until everything is soft.

Originally, this was eaten as a porridge, with a lump of butter. Now it is served as a stew.
Use of leftovers: Pour into a loaf pan; it will become hard enough to cut. Slice and serve cold.
Note: Originally, brown lentil-like beans were used. Use what you want: kidney beans, lentils, or some other beans.
Servings: 4 to 6.

SAILOR'S BEEF [MERIMIESPIHVI]

This tasty pot used to be served on Sundays—the day for whole-meat dishes.

1½ lbs beef, good quality chuck or
    round
1 tablespoon butter
1 tablespoon oil
2 large onions, sliced
1½ lbs potatoes, peeled and sliced

1½ teaspoon sea salt, or to taste
¼ teaspoon white pepper
½ cup water
½ cup light beer
2 tablespoons chopped parsley

Slice the meat thinly across the grain and make small (about 2 inches in diameter) steaks. Pound them on both sides with your knuckles. Combine the butter and oil, and brown the meat quickly in it. Drain, and set aside. Brown the onion in the same pan.

Preheat the oven to 350°F. Take a 3-quart ovenproof casserole with a lid, and put the potatoes, meat, and onions in it in layers. Sprinkle the layers with salt and pepper. Rinse the frying pan with ½ cup water, and pour over the pot. Pour in the beer. Cover and bake 2 hours. At the end, lower the heat if the pot seems to simmer too powerfully. Before serving, sprinkle with parsley.

Serve as a whole-meal dinner, with good bread to dip into the juice, and cucumber salad (see page 114).
Servings: 4 to 6.

LAMB AND CABBAGE POT [LAMMASKAALI]

Winter food—warm, strong, and comforting. It is a dish that one can have a terrible craving for if one is a cabbage fan.

3 lbs lean, boneless lamb (breast or
    shoulder)
½ tablespoon butter
1 cup water

1 large, firm, white head of winter
    cabbage
1 tablespoon sea salt
10 whole allspice, or ¼ teaspoon
    ground allspice

Cut the meat into 1-inch cubes. Brown them in the butter, and put them into a deep ovenproof pot with a lid. Rinse the pan with water, and pour over the meat.

Preheat the oven to 350°F. Cut the cabbage coarsely into 2-inch chunks and add to the meat. Add salt, pepper, and allspice, and stir. Let the pot simmer uncovered about ½ hour, enough for the top to brown.

Lower the heat to 200°F. Cover the pot, and let hatch 2 to 2½ hours.

Another method: It is common to brown the cabbage slowly before putting it into the pot, in the same way as for cabbage pie (see page 165). That way it is heavier and richer in calories.

Serve as a main course for dinner. Good when reheated.
Servings: 6 to 8.

LAMB AND TURNIP POT [LAMMASTA JA NAURISTA]

An Eva Mannerheim-Sparre recipe, with simple ingredients, but an elegant way of preparing them.

3 lbs lean, boneless lamb shoulder	¼ teaspoon white pepper, or to taste
2 tablespoons butter, or part butter and part oil	1 cup beef broth
2 tablespoons cognac	8–10 tiny white turnips, peeled
½ teaspoon sea salt	1 tablespoon raw sugar or honey

Preheat the oven to 350°F. Cut the lamb into 1-inch cubes. Brown them in half of the butter (or butter-oil mixture). When browned, remove the meat with a slotted spoon, carefully draining off all fat. Put the meat into an ovenproof pot with a lid. Sprinkle the meat with cognac, salt, and pepper. Pour the broth over. Cover, and let simmer 20 minutes. Lower the temperature to 225° and hatch 1½ to 2 hours.

Roll the turnips in the raw sugar or honey. Fry them in the rest of the butter until browned on all sides. Lift the turnips with a slotted spoon into the pot, draining off all fat. Mix, cover, and hatch 1 more hour.

Serve for dinner, with bread to dip, and a crisp, tart salad to lighten the meal. **Servings: 6.**

Chapter 6

FISH DISHES
[KALARUUAT]

Fish is loved all over Finland. Many of the fish that are commonly eaten in Finland are also well known in America. But some lake fish, like the Middle Finland favorite *muikku*, don't have American equivalents with a similar taste.

The most common and least expensive fish is the little cousin of herring, the Baltic Herring, *silakka*. Since it was often eaten because of its low price, no one dared boast of its culinary value. Only some time ago some devoted gastronomes started to praise its rather sweet, unique flavor: since then, the Baltic Herring has experienced a rise in status. Now many gourmet restaurants are proud to serve traditional as well as new Baltic Herring dishes. The American equivalent, smelt, is close in flavor, and can be used well in dishes that call for Baltic Herring.

Perch, pike, whitefish, and bream are also commonly used, and salmon is a beloved delicacy. I have given suggestions as to which fish to use in the recipes, but other fish, similar in taste and size, can be used as well. Only in smelt and salmon dishes would I not use substitutes.

PIKE IN EGG SAUCE [MUNAKASTIHAUKI]

This dill-flavored, sweet-and-sour sauce is delicious with pike, as well as with any other mild-flavored, white-fleshed fish. Try it with whiting or flounder.

2 cups water	1 teaspoon sea salt
1 carrot, scraped	1 pike or other fish (about 3 lbs,
1 bay leaf	when cleaned)

Sauce:

1½ cups broth reduced from boiling the fish	2 hard-boiled eggs, chopped
	1 tablespoon lemon juice
2 tablespoons unbleached white flour	½ teaspoon raw sugar or honey
¼ cup cold water	¼ cup chopped fresh dill leaves

Put the water, carrot, bay leaf, and half of the salt into a kettle that's large enough for boiling the fish. Bring to a boil, cover, and simmer about 10 minutes. Meanwhile, rub the inside of the fish with the rest of the salt.

Lower the heat until the water doesn't bubble any more. Put the fish into the water, cover the kettle, and simmer until the fish is done. Remove the fish carefully with slotted spoons, drain, and put on a serving platter, keep warm until serving.

To make the sauce: drain the cooking broth and discard the seasonings. Reduce the liquid to about 1½ cups. Mix the flour and cold water to make a smooth paste, and pour it into the broth, stirring well. Simmer about 5 minutes to let the sauce thicken. Add the chopped eggs, lemon juice, sugar or honey, and dill. Cover, and let stand about 10 minutes before serving. Reheat if necessary.

Another method: Instead of a whole fish, you may poach fish fillets, steaks, or frozen fish pieces, and serve the sauce over them.

Serve for a dinner with plain boiled potatoes. Cover the fish with the sauce, or serve from a separate bowl. Add a light green salad.

Servings: 4 to 6.

PIKE IN HORSERADISH SAUCE [PIPARJUURIHAUKI]

2 cups water	1 teaspoon sea salt
1 small onion, peeled	1 tablespoon butter
1 small carrot, scraped	1 tablespoon fresh horseradish,
2 whole allspice	grated
1 pike or other fish (about 3 lbs after cleaning)	

Sauce:

1½ cups broth from boiling the fish	2–3 tablespoons fresh horseradish, grated
2 tablespoons unbleached white flour	½ teaspoon raw sugar or honey
¼ cup cold water	

Put the water, onion, carrot, and allspice into a long fish kettle, cover, bring to a boil, and simmer about 10 minutes. Meanwhile, prepare the fish by rubbing it with salt inside and out. Put the butter and horseradish into the stomach of the fish.

Lower the heat so that the water doesn't bubble any more. Put the fish in water, spine side down. Cover, and simmer gently until done. With slotted spoons, remove the fish to a serving platter. Keep warm until serving.

To make the sauce, drain the broth, and discard the seasonings. Mix the flour and cold water to a smooth paste, pour it into the broth, and simmer about 5 minutes to let the sauce thicken. Add the horseradish and sugar or honey. Simmer 2 more minutes.

Another method: Instead of pike, use bream, whitefish, or whiting. Instead of a whole fish, poach fillets or steaks.

Serve for dinner with plain boiled potatoes or rice. Serve the sauce from a separate bowl. Decorate the fish with cucumber slices or lemon wedges and dill or parsley.

Servings: 4 to 6.

STUFFED PIKE [TÄYTETTY HAUKI]

This recipe goes back to the turn of the century. The prunes in the stuffing may seem surprising, but they are very good and very nutritious.

1 *pike or other fish (2½ to 3 lbs,*
when cleaned—leave the head on)

Stuffing:
1 *cup cooked brown rice*   6–8 *pitted prunes, soaked in water*
2 *hard-boiled eggs, chopped*   *until plump*
1 *tablespoon softened butter*

Topping:
1 *tablespoon butter*   ½ *teaspoon sea salt, or to taste*
1 *egg white, beaten*   ⅛ *teaspoon white pepper*
2 *tablespoons bread crumbs*

Dry the fish well. Mix together the rice, chopped eggs, and softened butter. Fill the stomach of the fish with this mixture. Arrange the prunes on top of the filling. Sew the stomach of the fish together. Pull the tail of the fish to touch the head, and join to form a circle.

Preheat the oven to 350°F. Grease an ovenproof glass casserole with half of the butter, and put the fish in it. Brush the fish with the egg white, sprinkle with bread crumbs, salt, and pepper. Dot with tiny lumps of the remaining butter. Bake the fish until done, 1 to 1½ hours. Test doneness by pulling a fin. If it feels loose, the fish should be done.

Serve for dinner with a light salad. Remove the sewing cord before serving.

Servings: 4 to 6.

DILLED FILLETS OF SMELTS [SILAKKAPIHVIT]

Rye flour is used to coat the fish before frying, and dill is used to give more aroma. This is one of the tastiest fish recipes I know.

½ cup rye flour
1 teaspoon sea salt
¼ teaspoon white pepper
1 egg, lightly beaten
2–3 tablespoons oil

1 tablespoon butter
2 lbs smelts, cleaned and butterflied
½ cup chopped fresh dill leaves

In a shallow bowl, mix together the rye flour, salt, and pepper. In another bowl, beat the egg lightly. Heat the mixture of oil and butter and keep it hot: do not let burn.

To make "sandwiches" of the butterflied fish, take two, face them and put together, skin sides out, with a generous amount of chopped dill between. Dip the fish "sandwiches" first in the egg, then in the rye flour. Coat on both sides.

Fry quickly in the hot oil-butter mixture, and drain on paper towels. The fish should be dark brown and crisp. Keep hot until serving time.

Serve with plain boiled or mashed potatoes, and pickled beets. You may sprinkle a little diluted vinegar over the fish.

Leftover fish: The fillets are also delicious cold. You may use them to fill sandwiches.

Servings: 4 to 6.

BROILED SMELTS [HIILISILAKAT]

The best way to cook the smelts is on a picnic grill made of wire, over hot coals.

1 lb smelts, insides and heads removed

1½–2 teaspoons sea salt
¼ cup oil

Salt water:
3 tablespoons sea salt

1 quart water

Rub the smelts with some salt, and brush them with oil on both sides. Put them in a row on a picnic grill and broil over hot coals; the smelts will get a bubbly, burned surface that makes them great. Or heat a broiling pan very, very hot, and broil the smelts in it.

Dissolve the salt in the water. Dip the smelts into salted water. Keep warm until serving. Best if served right away.

Serve with hot boiled potatoes. Use cold smelts on a sandwich.
Servings: 4.

BOILED SALMON [KEITETTY LOHI]

2–3 lbs small whole salmon, or piece   *Water to barely cover the fish*
   of salmon

For each quart of water use:
   3 *tablespoons white vinegar*   5 *whole white peppercorns*
   1 *tablespoon sea salt*   10 *strong stalks dill (reserve the*
   1 *onion, peeled and halved*   *leaves)*
   1 *bay leaf*

Put the water, vinegar, salt, onion, bay leaf, peppercorns, and dill into a saucepan. Cover, and bring to a boil. Simmer about 20 minutes. Remove from heat and let cool a little.

Place the salmon in a long fish kettle. Pour the cooled liquid over it, through a sieve, so that all of the seasonings are drained off. Cover partially, bring to a boil, then lower the heat so that the water merely simmers. Simmer until done, 30 to 45 minutes.

You may serve the fish warm or cold. If you serve it warm, remove from liquid, dry, and place on a serving platter. Keep warm until serving time. Reserve the liquid to make warm herb sauce.

If you serve the fish cold, let it cool in the liquid. Then remove, dry, and place on a serving platter. Keep chilled until serving time.

Serve either warm or cold as a main course. Decorate with dill leaves, lemon, and lettuce. Serve boiled smorgasbord potatoes (see page 106).

Warm Herb Sauce:
   1 *tablespoon butter*   2 *tablespoons finely chopped*
   2 *tablespoons unbleached white*   *chives*
      flour   2 *tablespoons finely chopped dill*
1½ *cups cooking liquid*   *leaves*
   2 *tablespoons finely chopped parsley*

Cook the butter and flour in a saucepan about 5 minutes. Add liquid little by little, stirring and letting simmer after each addition. After all liquid is added, simmer 5 minutes. Add parsley, chives, and dill.
   Servings: 4 to 6.

BAKED SALMON [PAISTETTU LOHI]

Salmon is one of those fine foods that taste best, when as little as possible is done to it.

4 salmon steaks, about 1 inch thick   Chopped dill
1 tablespoon melted butter   Lemon wedges
½ teaspoon sea salt

Preheat the oven to 450°F. Brush an oven pan lightly with butter, place the salmon steaks on it. Mix the salt and melted butter, and brush the tops of the steaks very lightly. Bake the steaks about 10 minutes. Remove from the oven.

Turn the broiler on as high as possible. Brush the steaks again with butter. Put them under the broiler for about 2 minutes a side, to take on an appetizing brown color. Turn the steaks carefully; do not pierce. After turning, brush the other side with butter.

Serve for dinner with steamed or creamed spinach (see page 111) or spinach casserole (see page 111). Sprinkle the steaks with dill and pass around the lemon.
Servings: 4.

FISH IN FOIL [FOLIOKALA]

1 small fish, cleaned   1 tablespoon dill leaves
½ teaspoon sea salt, or to taste   1 tablespoon butter
   Foil paper   1 teaspoon parsley
¼ carrot, sliced thin   Juice of ½ lemon
¼ scallion or less, sliced thin

Rub the fish with salt, inside and out. Let stand in a bowl about 15 minutes. Preheat the oven to 450°F.

Butter the inside of the foil and put the fish in the middle. Place the carrot and scallion slices around the fish. Put some dill and some butter into the stomach of the fish, and sprinkle the fish with the rest of the dill and the parsley, and dot with the rest of the butter. Sprinkle with lemon juice. Make a package of the foil, sealing the ends tightly. Bake the fish 20 to 30 minutes.

Another method: You may bake the package on any fire, in a hot frying pan, or in the hot ashes of a fireplace.
Servings: 1.

HERRING IN PAPER [PAPERISILLI]

This simple herring dish is a popular lunch, when one has a taste for something extra salty.

1 small salted herring, cleaned   2 tablespoons butter
  Milk or tea

Soak the herring for a couple of hours in milk or tea. Dry well. Butter a sheet of aluminum foil, put the herring in the middle, and dot with the rest of the butter. Wrap the herring into a tight package.

Heat an ungreased frying pan very hot. Put the foil package into it, and cook, turning the package once. A small herring should take about 10 minutes to a side.

Lift the whole package to your plate, and open. Serve with hot boiled potatoes and pickled beets.
Servings: 1.

DILL-FLAVORED CRAYFISH [RAVUT]

Eating crayfish in August is a ritual in Scandinavia. Boiling crayfish is also a ritual, and there is only one correct way—no arguing about it.

Crayfish freshly caught (about 10
per person)

For each quart of water use:
1 oz coarse sea salt   Dill stalks with the crowns
1 teaspoon raw sugar

The crayfish must be alive when boiled. Keep them in sea water until cooking time. If you serve them in the evening, make them in the morning so they will have time to marinate in the cooking liquid.

To wash the crayfish well, grab them on the back, and brush under running water.

Put the water, salt, and sugar into a large, deep kettle. There should be enough water to cover all the crayfish. Add the dill stalks and reserve the leaves for decoration. (Leaves will make the water slimy and green.) If you do not have crown dill, add 1 teaspoon dill seeds to each quart of water.

Bring the water to a boil, and let simmer 5 minutes. Put the crayfish into the water, and raise the heat to keep the water bubbling. Cover the pot and simmer 10 to 15 minutes. If the crayfish was alive, it turns red. Discard any that don't. Also, the tails of the crayfish will turn down. Discard any whose tail stays straight. Do not overcook. The crayfish are done when there is a crack between the body and the turned-down tail.

With a slotted spoon, lift the crayfish from water. Drain the water, discard all the dill stalks, and pour the water back into the kettle. Lift the crayfish back into water, and let them cool in it. Cover the surface of the kettle with more dill crowns or leaves. Chill.

In the evening, remove from the marinade, and arrange the crayfish on a large platter. Decorate with dill crowns and leaves.

Serve with crisp warm toast and butter. The crayfish meat will be placed on buttered toast, eaten, and rinsed down with chilled white wine or iced schnapps. At each place put a finger bowl filled with cold water, freshened with a lemon wedge or black currant leaves. Everyone needs a bib and a lot of paper napkins. In Finland the fun lasts until the small hours. For a late snack, a cheese tray with fruit is served, or Jansson's Temptation (see page 62).

DILLED SHRIMP

For those who don't have crayfish readily available, I have used a similar recipe for shrimp.

1 quart water	1 teaspoon dill seeds
1 tablespoon coarse sea salt	1 lb medium shrimp
1 teaspoon raw sugar	
1 large bunch fresh dill, leaves removed	

Start in the morning. Put the water, salt, sugar, dill stalks and seed into a deep kettle, bring to a boil and simmer, covered, for 15 minutes. Put the shrimp in, cover, and simmer 2 to 3 minutes, or until the shrimp are done. Remove from the liquid, drain off the dill, and put the shrimp back in the liquid.

Chill until evening. Serve as you would crayfish.

Servings: 2 to 3.

Chapter 7

MEAT DISHES
[LIHARUUAT]

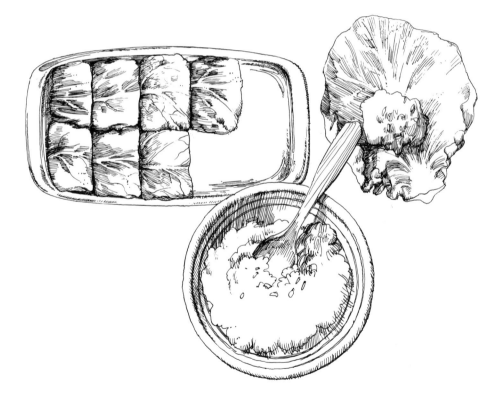

Whole-meat dishes, even when I was a child, were mostly reserved for Sunday and weekend treats. Only with the rise of the standard of living has meat become more common. Still, the best Finnish recipes are the ones in which meats are mixed with other ingredients.

Pork was in the old times the most common meat in the Finnish diet, and there are still a good number of pork recipes available. Lamb used to be more common than it is now, whereas beef was more rare.

Chicken, until about 20 years ago, was considered a special Sunday meat; only lately, with the increased production of broilers, has it become as common and inexpensive a meat as in America. That is why there aren't any really original chicken recipes: most have been adopted very recently from other cuisines.

Ground meat, liver, kidneys, and especially blood have always had a place in the menu.

Reindeer meat is a specialty, and is transported from Lapland to the southern gourmet's table. I have included one reindeer recipe as an example.

Most of the meat dishes in this book are ones that are common every-day dishes even today. There is much Russian influence that is easily traced; some of the dishes are commonly known in all Scandinavia. In some dishes one can see the influence of some other foreign kitchen, for example, that of Germany or France. But all of the foods have acquired a specific Finnish flavor, and have been known and made in this way for years.

PORK SAUCE [LÄSKIKASTIKE]

This used to be a once-a-week dish, and one of the few meat dishes available. It's been pushed away to make room for more elegant dishes, but I must have it once in a while, for old time's sake, and for the wonderful taste.

½ lb meaty bacon or salt pork, sliced ¼ inch thick	2½ cups water
2–3 tablespoons rye flour	1 teaspoon sea salt, or to taste

Cut the bacon into about 1-inch pieces. Fry the pieces in a heavy frying pan, so that they become brown and crisp. Sprinkle with the rye flour, stir, and fry the flour until evenly brown, but not burned.

Add the water a little at a time, stirring and letting simmer after each addition. Season with salt. Let the sauce simmer 20 to 30 minutes, or until it becomes smooth, brown, and shiny, and acquires a deep pork taste. It should also reduce.

Serve with mashed potatoes or rutabaga casserole (see page 108). Make a little well in the middle of the mashed vegetable, fill it with the sauce, and enjoy. Add cucumber salad (see page 114), or a light green salad.
Servings: 4 to 6.

FRIED PORK [TIRRIPAISTI]

In these anti-cholesterol days this dish can't belong to the regular menu. But eaten only occasionally, it's a treat.

1½ lbs pork butt, in large 1-inch thick slices	1 teaspoon sea salt
	1 cup water

Brown the pork slices slowly in a large, heavy frying pan so that the fat melts and browns. Brown on both sides. Sprinkle with salt, and pour the water over.

Cover the pan, and simmer the pork over low heat 1 to 1½ hours. The juice should be strong and tasty, and somewhat reduced.

Eat on a cold day with a grated salad. Serve thick slices of bread to dip into the juice.
Servings: 4 to 6.

BACON CAKES [SILAVAKAKUT]

These pancakes are known in all of Scandinavia. Although originally a lunch dish, they are good for an especially hearty breakfast.

1 lb potatoes	1 teaspoon sea salt
1 egg, beaten lightly	½ teaspoon raw sugar or honey
½ cup unbleached white flour	

Filling:
*¼ lb meaty bacon, chopped and
    browned*

Boil the potatoes in their jackets, peel and mash while hot. Let cool. Add the beaten egg, flour, salt, and sugar or honey. Make a soft dough, firm enough to handle.

Wet your hands with cold water before handling the dough. Take a handful, and form it into a ball. Press the middle with your thumb, fill the hole with bacon. Cover the hole. Flatten the ball.

You may either boil or fry the cakes. To boil; drop the cakes into boiling, salted water, let them sink, and simmer until they pop to the surface. Or fry them in oil or butter in a pancake pan.

Serve for lunch or breakfast, with lingonberry or cranberry preserves.
Servings: 4 to 6.

OLD-FASHIONED PORK ROAST
[VANHAN AJAN PORSAANPAISTI]

To make this the real old-fashioned way, you should start 3 or 4 days before. The roast will be slightly sweet, with the aroma of cloves and cinnamon.

*1 pork roast, about 6 lbs
1 cup corn syrup or molasses
2 tablespoons sea salt
1 tablespoon crushed white
    peppercorns*

*1 tablespoon crushed allspice
3 tablespoons prepared mustard
1 teaspoon cinnamon
20 whole cloves
1 cup bread crumbs*

Rub the pork roast with a mixture of corn syrup or molasses, salt, crushed peppercorns, and allspice. Rub on all sides. Put into a deep dish, and let stand in a cold place 3 to 4 days. Twice a day spoon the juice that forms at the bottom of the bowl over the roast.

Remove from the marinade, and dry. Preheat the oven to 325°F. Mix together the mustard and cinnamon. Rub it into the surface of the pork. Stud the roast with the whole cloves. Sprinkle with the bread crumbs. Bake in the oven 3 to 3½ hours. Place a large pot full of boiling water at the bottom of the oven.

Serve with plain accompaniments: potatoes, bread, pickles.
Servings: 8 to 10.

GRANDMA'S BAKED HAM [MUMMON JOULUKINKKU]

This old way of baking the Christmas ham is one which my grandmother favored. The children got the hard rye crust to chew on and to dip into the gravy; it was good for teeth, and helpful for the special kind of Christmas hunger.

1 ham, about 10 lbs

Crust:
3 cups water   *7 cups rye flour*

Preheat the oven to 325°F. Mix the water and rye flour to make a hard, stiff dough. With wet hands, make a ball of the dough, flatten it, and cover the ham with it. It should cover the top and sides of the ham. Put the ham in a heavy oven pan. Pour about 1 cup water into it.

You may count on about ½ hour per pound baking time for the ham. The baking usually takes 5 to 6 hours. At the end, you may cover the dough with foil to prevent burning. Add water to the pan so the fat doesn't burn.

After taking the ham out of the oven, let it sit and calm down for 10 minutes. Remove the crust, and wrap it in foil to make it a little softer. Slice the ham.

Christmas ham is served with rutabaga (see page 108) or sweetened potato casserole (see page 107), stewed peas (see page 112), boiled prunes, pickled onions (see page 118), rosolli (see page 18), and mustard. Serve the softened crust like bread, and dip it into the gravy. Use leftovers for cold cuts and soups.

Servings: 10 or more.

FINNISH STROGANOFF [STROGANOFF]

A close relative to the original Russian dish, the Finnish version is much stronger and stewier than the stroganoff known in America.

2–2½ lbs boneless stewing beef, cut into 1-inch cubes
2 tablespoons butter, or a mixture of butter and oil
1 onion, chopped
1 tablespoon unbleached white flour

1 cup water or beef broth
2–3 tablespoons tomato puree
1 teaspoon prepared mustard
¼ teaspoon white pepper
1 small dill pickle
¼ cup sour cream (optional)

Brown the meat in half of the butter, then lift with a slotted spoon to a heavy pot (cast-iron pot or a flameproof casserole). Brown the onion, and spoon it over the meat.

Add more butter to the pan, brown the flour in it until strongly colored, but not burned. Add the water or broth to the pan gradually, stirring and letting simmer after each addition. Let the sauce thicken. Add tomato puree, mustard, and pepper. Pour the sauce over the meat, stir.

Cover the pot, and simmer over very low heat about 2 hours. Cut the pickle into tiny cubes and add to the sauce. Check the salt. Before serving, add sour cream, if wanted.

Serve with boiled rice or macaroni.
Servings: 4 to 6.

BEEF WITH HORSERADISH [PIPARJUURILIHA]

2–2½ lbs boneless brisket, flanken, or any cut good for boiling
4–5 cups water
2 teaspoons sea salt
1 small onion, peeled

1 small carrot, scraped
1 bay leaf
5 whole white peppercorns
3 whole cloves

Sauce:

2 cups of the boiling liquid
2 tablespoons unbleached white
flour
3 tablespoons lemon juice

½ teaspoon raw sugar or honey
2–4 tablespoons grated fresh
horseradish

Accompaniment:
2 tablespoons grated fresh
horseradish

Combine the water, salt, onion, carrot, bay leaf, peppercorns, and cloves in a large kettle. Bring to a boil and simmer, covered, about 5 minutes. Put the meat in the water, bring to a boil, and simmer until foam rises to the surface. Skim off the foam.

Lower the heat, cover the kettle, and simmer until the meat is done, 1 to 1½ hours.

Remove the meat from the kettle, drain, and slice thin. Arrange the slices on a serving dish. You may have the meat either warm or cold. Sprinkle with horseradish.

To make the sauce, drain the cooking liquid, and discard the seasonings. Use 2 cups for the sauce; save the remaining liquid for soups. Heat the liquid. Add the flour mixed with a little cold water, stir well, and let simmer until the sauce thickens. Add lemon juice, sugar or honey, and horseradish. Serve from a separate bowl.

Carrot casserole (see page 110), spinach casserole (see page 111), and fresh grated vegetables are good dishes to accompany. Serve cold leftover meat on sandwiches.
Servings: 4 to 6.

BEEF A LA LINDSTRÖM [LINDSTRÖMIN PIHVI]

The Swedes also know Lindström; it is a popular everyday dish, made with any ground beef, and "something better" made with a better cut, for occasions.

1 lb lean ground beef
1 large boiled potato, mashed
2 small boiled beets, grated
1 small or ½ medium dill pickle,
chopped
¼ cup light cream

1 teaspoon sea salt
¼ teaspoon white pepper
1 egg
1 onion, cut into rings and fried
in oil

Mix together the ground beef, potato, beets, and chopped pickle. Add the cream, salt, and pepper, mix well. Beat the egg and add to the mixture. Stir until it starts to stick to the bowl.

Make 4 to 6 round patties. Either fry them in oil on both sides, or broil them. Brown the onion rings and serve on top.

Serve for lunch or dinner with mashed potatoes.
Servings: 4 to 6 patties.

FINNISH SAUERBRATEN [HAPANPAISTI]

This dish is obviously adopted from the German cuisine, but it has developed a distinctive Finnish character of its own.

1 roast beef, 5–5½ lbs

Marinade:
8 cups light beer
2 cups white or cider vinegar
2 teaspoons cracked white peppercorns
1 teaspoon cracked allspice
1 piece ginger or 1 teaspoon ground ginger

Oil for frying
1 cup brown sugar or dark honey
20 juniper berries (the original recipe also calls for a few tiny juniper twigs)
1 tablespoon grated horseradish

Start 3 to 4 days before serving. In a large, deep bowl—earthenware, not metal—combine the beer, vinegar, pepper, allspice, ginger, sugar or honey, juniper berries, and horseradish. Stir well until the sugar has dissolved. Put the roast into the marinade: the marinade should just cover the roast. Cover the bowl, refrigerate, and let marinate 3 to 4 days.

Drain off the marinade and dry the meat. Preheat the oven to 350°F. In a large, heavy iron pot or Dutch oven, brown the roast on all sides in oil. Pour off most of the oil. Pour about ½ cup of the marinade around the roast. Cover the Dutch oven, and bake about 1½ hours for medium rare. Check the liquid a couple of times and add more if necessary. There should always be about 1 inch of liquid at the bottom. Do not lift the cover too often.

The meat itself will be tart and spicy, so serve it with plain and simple accompaniments: bread, mashed potatoes, salad.
Servings: 8 to 10.

FINNISH STEAK TARTARE [TARTARPIHVI]

This is a popular restaurant dish, considered an energy pack that will also restore one's spirits. Distinctly Finnish in its presentation, it differs from the American anchovies-and-seasoned-sauce version by emphasizing the meat taste more. You must have an excellent cut of meat for this.

2 lbs very lean ground top round or top sirloin (see Note)
4 raw egg yolks
4 small boiled or pickled beets, chopped

2 dill pickles, chopped
4 tablespoons capers
½ cup finely chopped onion
Parsley

Make 4 square patties of the ground meat. Put each in the middle of a plate. Decorate the surface by pressing across each with a sharp knife. From tiny individual bowls for each condiment, serve each guest the egg yolks, beets, pickles, onions, and capers. Decorate with parsley. Put out the salt shaker and peppermill.

To mix the steak, first, chop lightly across it with your knife. Pour the yolk over, break it, and chop it into the meat. Sprinkle with ground pepper and some salt. (The pickles will provide salt as well.) Put the other ingredients on the steak and keep chopping until adequately mixed.

Often the steak is served with a slice of whole-rye bread. Nothing more is needed: it's enough for lunch or dinner, healthy, pure, and satisfying.

Note: Purists claim that the only way to make steak tartare is to scrape the meat with a sharp knife, not grind it. But if the meat is good, strong, and juicy, it will be fine if ground.

Servings: 4.

CABBAGE ROLLS [KAALIKÄÄRYLEET]

This dish has been a loved one in Finland for years.

1 *medium head of cabbage*	1 *teaspoon marjoram leaves,*
Water	*crushed*
Salt	¼ *teaspoon white pepper*
1 *lb ground beef*	¼ *teaspoon sea salt*
1½ *cups cooked barley or brown*	1 *tablespoon molasses*
rice (cooked in broth)	1–2 *tablespoons butter (or butter*
2 *tablespoons cream*	*and oil)*
1 *teaspoon sea salt*	¼ *cup water*

Boil the cabbage head in lightly salted water until the leaves become transparent, about 10 minutes. Drain well. Remove 15 of the larger outer leaves carefully so that they stay whole. These you use to wrap the filling in.

For the filling, mix together the meat, barley or rice, cream, salt, marjoram, and pepper. Chop some of the inside leaves of the cabbage finely, and add about 1 cup to the filling.

To make the rolls, cut the thick stems of the large cabbage leaves a little thinner. Put about 2 tablespoons of the filling in the middle of the leaf and wrap it into a tight little square package. Wrap like any package: first one end, then the sides, and then roll. Grease a shallow oven casserole or glass oven pan. Put the rolls in it tightly side by side, seam side down.

Preheat the oven to 350°F. Sprinkle the rolls with salt and pour the molasses over them. Dot with tiny lumps of butter and pour the water into the bottom of the pan. Bake 1½ to 2 hours. Every now and then, spoon some of the pan juice over them. If the rolls get dry, add a little more water or molasses.

Serve as a main course with lingonberry or cranberry preserves. Cabbage rolls are very good when reheated.

Servings: 4 to 6.

VEAL STEW [VASIKANVIILLOKKI]

2–2½ lbs boneless veal shoulder
   4 cups water
   1 onion

1 carrot, scraped
1 teaspoon sea salt
¼ teaspoon ginger

Sauce:
   2 cups of the cooking liquid
   3 tablespoons unbleached white
     flour
   ¼ cup cold water
   3 tablespoons lemon juice or
     vinegar

1 teaspoon raw sugar or honey
Pinch of ginger
Salt, if necessary
1 tablespoon butter (optional)

Bring the water to a boil, add the onion, carrot, salt, and ginger. Cover and simmer 10 minutes, then lower the heat. Put in the whole piece of veal. Cover and simmer about 1 hour, or until the meat is just done. (Turn the veal over once; be sure not to pierce it.)

Take the veal out. Drain and reserve the cooking liquid. Cut the veal into cubes of about 1½ inches. Keep warm.

Reduce the cooking liquid a little. Use about 2 cups for the sauce: save the rest for soups. Put the 2 cups into a saucepan and heat. Mix the flour into the cold water to make a smooth paste and pour slowly into the hot broth, stirring well with a wire whisk. Simmer about 10 minutes and let thicken. Season with lemon juice or vinegar, sugar or honey, and ginger. Check salt. Add butter for a richer but more fattening sauce.

Put the meat pieces into a kettle, pour the sauce over them. Stir and cover. Simmer about 1 hour, or until the meat pieces are soft and stew-like.

Serve with rice, spinach casserole (see page 111), or carrot casserole (see page 110), and with a tart, bright-colored salad.

Leftover broth: Use for mushroom soup (see page 55), or any other delicate soup that calls for broth.

Servings: 4 to 6.

MEAT WITH DILL [TILLILIHA]

Meat with dill is one of those popular dishes now sold both canned and frozen in Finland.

  3–4 cups water
    1 teaspoon sea salt
10–15 strong dill stalks
     (reserve the leaves)

2–2½ lbs lean, boneless lamb or veal
    shoulder

Sauce:
   2 cups of the cooking liquid
   3 tablespoons unbleached white
     flour
   ¼ cup cold water

2 tablespoons white vinegar
2 tablespoons raw sugar or honey
1/3 cup finely chopped dill leaves

Bring the water to a boil, add the dill stalks and salt. Cover and simmer about 10 minutes. Lower the heat and put the meat in. Cover and simmer until the meat is done, 1 to 1½ hours.

Remove the meat and cut it into 1½-inch cubes. Keep warm. Drain and reserve the liquid. Reduce it somewhat. Use 2 cups for the sauce, and save the rest for other uses. Put the 2 cups of broth into a saucepan. Heat. Mix the flour and cold water into a smooth paste and pour slowly into the broth, stirring all the time with a wire whisk. Simmer about 10 minutes. Add the vinegar, sugar or honey, and dill leaves.

Pour the sauce over the meat cubes. Cover and simmer 40 minutes to 1 hour, or until the meat is soft and stew-like.

Serve with mashed or boiled potatoes and pickled beets (see page 117), or a grated salad.
Servings: 4 to 6.

GRANDMA'S LEG OF LAMB [MUMMON LAMPAANPAISTI]

4–5 *lbs leg of lamb*
1 *tablespoon good mustard*
8–10 *small white onions*
6–8 *carrots, scraped*
8–10 *small potatoes, peeled*

1 *tablespoon sea salt, or to taste*
1 *cup strong coffee*
1 *teaspoon sugar*
Cream

Sauce:
Juice from the pan, about 1½ cups
1 *tablespoon unbleached white flour, mixed in ¼ cup water*

1 *teaspoon mustard*

Preheat the oven to 425°F. Rub the surface of the lamb with mustard. Put the leg of lamb onto a heavy baking pan. Arrange the onions, carrots, and potatoes around it. Bake in the oven 15 minutes, or until the surface has become brown. Take out and lower the heat to 325°F.

Rub the lamb with salt. Make a cup of coffee with sugar and cream. Pour the coffee over the lamb and put the pan back into the oven.

Bake about 2 hours; it should be slightly pink in the middle. Or use a meat thermometer for desired doneness. Every 20 minutes check the liquid in the pan and spoon it over the lamb and vegetables. Add water if necessary. Turn the vegetables a couple of times. Do not let them burn.

Remove the lamb from the oven. Cover it with a sheet of foil and let sit 15 minutes to make it easier to cut and keep the juices in.

Meanwhile, to make the sauce, pour the liquid from the oven pan into a saucepan, through a sieve. Add water, if necessary, to make about 1½ cups. Bring to a boil. Mix the flour and water into a smooth paste and pour into the saucepan, whisking well all the time. Simmer until it thickens. Season with mustard, check the salt.

Slice the roast and serve surrounded by the vegetables. Serve sauce separately. Add black currant jelly or mint jelly to the table.
Leftover bone: Use it for soups.
Servings: 6 to 8.

REINDEER HASH [PORONKÄRISTYS]

In Lapland this is an everyday dish for reindeermen, cooked often over open fires. The frozen reindeer meat is shaved paper thin from big hunks of meat. In the south the dish is a delicacy, made from commercially packaged frozen reindeer shavings.

1 lb frozen reindeer meat	*Salt to taste*
½ lb bacon, cut into cubes	*1–1½ cups water*

If the meat is in 1 piece, scrape it thinly across the grain. Melt the bacon in a heavy iron pot or frying pan. Add the reindeer meat and brown until the fat starts to boil on the surface.

Add enough water just to cover the meat. Season with salt. Cover partially, and let hatch an hour or 2. Add a little more water if necessary.

Serve as an exotic dinner dish, with loose mashed potatoes and mashed fresh lingonberries or cranberries.
Servings: 4.

LIVER-CARROT STROGANOFF
[MAKSA-PORKKANASTROGANOFF]

The combination of liver, carrots, and parsley supplies a load of vitamins and iron. This is a fairly modern recipe.

3 medium carrots, scraped and diced	*1 tablespoon unbleached white flour*
1 cup water	*½ teaspoon sea salt, or to taste*
2 lbs beef liver, cut into 1-inch cubes	*¼ teaspoon white or black pepper*
1 tablespoon butter	*¼ teaspoon marjoram or rosemary*
1 tablespoon vegetable oil	*leaves, crushed*
1 medium onion, chopped	*¼ cup chopped fresh parsley*

Boil or steam the carrot cubes, using about 1 cup water, until almost done. Drain, and reserve the cooking liquid. Put the carrots into a saucepan.

In a heavy frying pan, brown the cubed liver quickly in a mixture of oil and butter. The surface of the liver should become dark brown and crisp, but the inside should stay tender-pink. Put the liver pieces on top of the carrots. Then brown the onion, and add to the saucepan. Cover the pan.

Brown the flour in the frying pan until dark brown, but not burned. Add the carrot boiling water, a little at a time, stirring well and letting simmer after each addition. Pour the sauce into the saucepan through a dense sieve. You should have just enough sauce to "tie together" the liver and carrots. Do not drown them.

Add salt, pepper, and marjoram or rosemary. Cover the pot and let simmer over very low heat about 10 minutes. Before serving, add parsley.

Serve with boiled or mashed potatoes, or rice.
Servings: 4 to 6.

GROUND LIVER PATTIES [JAUHEMAKSAPIHVIT]

1½ lbs beef or pork liver, ground
½ lb raw potatoes, peeled and grated
   or ground
1 onion, finely chopped

1½ teaspoons sea salt
¼ teaspoon white pepper
2 tablespoons oil, or butter and oil

Mix the liver, grated potatoes, chopped onion, salt, and pepper. Mix into a rather loose dough. If you have a pancake pan with small rings, fry the patties in it. Otherwise, form round patties with your hands and fry them in oil or a mixture of butter and oil.

Preheat the oven to 350°F. After frying, place the patties in an oven pan and cover with foil. Let bake in the oven 15 minutes. It will soften the potatoes and keep the patties juicy.

Serve with boiled or mashed potatoes and lingonberry or cranberry preserves.
Servings: 6 to 8 patties.

STEWED KIDNEYS [MUNUAISMUHENNOS]

2 lbs fresh beef kidneys
1 tablespoon butter, or butter and oil
2 tablespoons unbleached white flour
1 cup water or beef broth

1 tablespoon wine or cider vinegar
½ teaspoon sea salt
⅛ teaspoon white pepper
2 tablespoons chopped parsley

Clean the kidneys and remove all the fat and membranes. Chop into small cubes. Brown the cubes in butter or a mixture of butter and oil. Sprinkle with flour and stir to let the flour brown. Add the water or broth, a little at a time; stirring and letting simmer after each addition. Add the vinegar, salt, and pepper.

Cover the pan, reduce heat, and simmer slowly 20 minutes. Sprinkle with parsley before serving.

Serve on a bed of rice or barley with a fresh salad.
Servings: 4 to 6.

FRIED LAMB KIDNEYS [PAISTETUT LAMPAANMUNUAISET]

The recipe is by Eva Mannerheim-Sparre, which means simple-but-elegant.

4 cups water	⅛ teaspoon white pepper
2 lbs lamb kidneys	2 tablespoons lemon juice
2 tablespoons butter	1 teaspoon prepared mustard
½ teaspoon sea salt	

Bring the water to a boil. Drop the kidneys into the boiling water for 2 minutes. Take out and drain.

Split the kidneys in half. Brown half of the butter in a frying pan and fry the kidneys on both sides, 4 minutes to a side. Sprinkle with salt and pepper. Put on a serving platter and keep warm.

Add the lemon juice to the pan. Stir in the mustard and the rest of the butter. Pour the juice over the kidneys.

Serve on a bed of rice or with toast.
Servings: 4.

BLOOD PANCAKES [VERILETUT]

1 small onion, chopped	1 egg
1 tablespoon butter	2 tablespoons sea salt, or to taste
1½ cups fresh blood	¼ teaspoon white pepper, or to taste
1½ cups light beer	½ teaspoon marjoram, crushed
1/3 cup rye flour	2–3 tablespoons oil, or butter and oil,
1/3 cup barley flour	for frying

White Onion Sauce:

2 medium-size onions, chopped	1½ cups milk
2 tablespoons butter	⅛ teaspoon white pepper
2 tablespoons unbleached white flour	½ teaspoon sea salt

Brown the onion in the butter and let cool.

Pour the blood into a mixing bowl through a sieve. Beat it for a while with a wire whisk until thin strings form and the blood turns lighter in color. Add the beer, and beat. Add fried onion, rye flour, barley flour, and egg, beating well to keep the batter smooth. Add salt, pepper, and marjoram.

Heat a pancake pan with small rings, and grease the rings. Pour them about 2/3 full of the batter, and fry the pancakes on both sides until crisp and brown. Keep warm until serving time.

To make the sauce, cook the onion in butter until tender and transparent. Sprinkle with flour, stir, and cook a couple of minutes. Do not brown. Add the milk little by little, stirring well after each addition. Simmer 5 to 10 minutes, or until thick and creamy. Season with salt and pepper.

Serve the blood pancakes with lingonberry or cranberry preserves. You may add boiled potatoes and white onion sauce.
Servings: 4 to 6.

Chapter 8

VEGETABLE MAIN DISHES
[VIHANNESRUUAT]

Most of these dishes have nothing to do with the vegetarian ideology; they were simply developed as substitutes for high-priced meat dishes. They can well be used today for the same reason, or just for variety's sake. Some dishes can as well be used as vegetable side dishes, with fish or meat.

The mushroom dishes are considered delicacies, especially those made of the two prized mushrooms, the chantarelle and the morelle. These can be bought canned in America, and are worth trying in that form for special occasions.

SPINACH PANCAKES [PINAATTIOHUKKAAT]

¾–1 lb spinach
1 cup water
1 egg
1¾ cups unbleached white flour
1 cup sour cream

1 teaspoon sea salt
½ teaspoon raw sugar
2 tablespoons melted butter, or oil
Butter and oil, for frying

Wash the spinach leaves, put into a saucepan, and cover with water. Cover the pan, bring to a boil, and simmer about 5 minutes, or until the spinach is limp. Drain the spinach and reserve the liquid. Chop the spinach fine.

Beat the egg lightly and add the spinach cooking liquid. Beat in the flour and sour cream in turns. Add salt, sugar, and melted butter or oil. Stir in spinach. The dough should be nicely green.

In a small-ring pancake pan or a crêpe pan, fry rather thick pancakes on both sides, until crisp and brown. Keep warm until serving time.
   Another method: Make nettle pancakes in the same way.

Serve as a main course, with melted butter, and cranberry or lingonberry preserves.
   Servings: 4 to 6.

CARROT PANCAKES [PORKKANAOHUKKAAT]

½ *cup bread crumbs*
¾ *cup milk, or light cream*
2 *eggs*
2 *cups grated carrots*
¼ *cup unbleached white flour*

1 *tablespoon vegetable oil or melted*
   butter
1 *teaspoon sea salt, or to taste*
   Oil or butter for frying

Soak the bread crumbs in the milk or light cream. Separate the eggs. Mix together grated carrots, milk and bread crumbs, flour, egg yolks, and oil or melted butter. Season with salt. Beat the egg whites until stiff and fold in.

Heat a pancake pan or a heavy frying pan. With a spoon, drop on the hot greased pan small pancake-size patties and fry them on both sides, until done through.
   Another method: Deep fry the batter in oil, by dropping a spoonful of the batter in, as if making doughnuts.
Or bake the batter in ovenproof casserole at 350°F about ½ hour, as a pudding.

Serve the pancakes with brown rice. Serve the doughnuts as a snack. The pudding may be either a main course or a vegetable side dish.
   Servings: 4 to 6.

POTATO PANCAKES [PERUNAOHUKKAAT]

1 *egg*
1 *cup milk*
1 *cup grated raw potatoes*

½ *cup unbleached white flour*
1 *teaspoon sea salt*
   Oil or butter

Beat the egg lightly. Add milk, potatoes, flour, and salt. Beat well. Cover the bowl and let stand 1 hour.

Fry the pancakes in oil or butter in a pancake pan with small rings, or a regular frying pan. The pancakes should be brown and crisp. Keep hot until serving.

Serve for lunch with lingonberry or cranberry preserves, or as a hearty breakfast with bacon.
   Servings: 4.

PEA CHOPS [HERNEKYLJYKSET]

2 cups split peas	1/3 cup bread crumbs
1½ cups water	2/3 cup milk
1 boiled potato	2 eggs
2 boiled carrots	¼ teaspoon white pepper, or
1 tablespoon chopped onion	to taste
3–4 tablespoons vegetable oil	½ teaspoon sea salt, or to taste

Soak the peas and cook in water until soft and mushy. Add more water, if necessary. Grind or grate the potato and carrots. Fry the onion in oil. Soak the bread crumbs in milk.

Combine all the ingredients. If the mixture seems too stiff, add a little water. Shape about 6 round patties. Sprinkle them with bread crumbs and fry in oil on both sides.

Serve as a main course.
Servings: 4 to 6.

CELERY ROOT STEAKS [SELLERIPIHVIT]

2 medium-size celery roots	1 egg
1 cup water	¼ cup bread crumbs
½ teaspoon sea salt	3–4 tablespoons oil

Choose celery roots that do not seem stringy: the older and larger ones often have wooden strings that make them unpleasant to eat. Peel the celery roots, and slice into ½-inch thick slices.

Bring the salted water to a boil, and add celery slices. Lower the heat, cover, and simmer until done, about 20 minutes, but do not overcook. Or instead, steam the celery about 30 minutes.

Remove, drain, and cool a little. Beat the egg lightly. Dip the celery in egg, then roll in bread crumbs. Fry in oil on both sides until crisp. Drain on paper towels. Keep warm.

A light lunch dish, with a tart salad. Also good for a vegetable side dish.
Servings: 4.

BEET STEAKS [PUNAJUURIPIHVIT]

4 large beets, boiled until almost done   Oil
1 egg, beaten lightly   1 onion, sliced and separated into
¼ cup bread crumbs   rings

Peel and slice the beets into ½-inch thick slices. Dip the slices in egg, then roll in bread crumbs. Fry in oil on both sides. Keep warm.

Fry the onion rings in the oil, remove and drain. Put them on top of the beet steaks.

Serve as a main course with potatoes or steamed rice, and maybe a beet green sauce (see below).
Servings: 4.

BEET GREEN SAUCE [PUNAJUURENVARSIKASTIKE]

½ lb beet greens   1½ cups milk
1 cup water   ½ cup boiling liquid
1 tablespoon butter   ½ teaspoon sea salt
2 tablespoons unbleached white   Pinch of raw sugar, or honey
  flour

Rinse the beet greens well with cold water. Put them in a saucepan, cover with water, and bring to a boil. Simmer until the greens are limp, about 10 minutes. Take out the greens and reserve the liquid. Chop the greens fine.

In a saucepan, melt the butter, add flour, and cook but do not brown, about 5 minutes. Add the milk little by little, stirring and letting thicken after each addition. Add the boiling liquid and beet greens. Simmer 5 minutes. Add salt and sugar.

Serve over potatoes or rice, or with such meat dishes as Beef a la Lindström (see page 87) or ground liver patties (see page 93).
Servings: 4 to 6.

CABBAGE BALLS [KAALIPULLAT]

¾ lb cabbage   3 tablespoons bread crumbs
  Water   1 teaspoon sea salt
1 egg, lightly beaten   ¼ teaspoon white pepper
1 teaspoon unbleached white flour   Oil or butter
1 teaspoon potato starch

Steam the cabbage until it's soft, but not mushy. Chop it very fine or put it through a food mill.

Mix together the cabbage, egg, flour, potato starch, bread crumbs, salt, and pepper. Mix well. Using two spoons, take out small balls—like meat balls—and fry them in butter or oil, or a mixture of both. Remove from the pan and keep warm.

Serve with boiled potatoes with lingonberry or cranberry preserves.
Servings: 4 to 6.

CREAMED CHANTARELLES [KANTARELLIMUHENNOS]

Chantarelles are one of the most subtly delicate mushrooms and are popular in Finland as the first mushrooms of the fall. They can be bought in cans in the United States.

1 cup chantarelles (canned)
2 tablespoons butter
2½ tablespoons unbleached white
  flour
1 cup liquid from the can (add water,
  if needed)
1/5 cup cream
¼ cup chopped fresh dill leaves
½ teaspoon sea salt, or to taste
⅛ teaspoon white pepper, or to taste
  Pinch of raw sugar

Drain the chantarelles well, and reserve the liquid. Melt the butter in a saucepan, and cook the chantarelles in it, for about 5 minutes, but do not brown. Sprinkle the chantarelles with the flour, stir, and cook a couple of minutes.

Add the liquid little by little, stirring well after each addition. After all the liquid has been added, add the cream. Stir in the chopped dill. Simmer the sauce until it becomes thick and creamy. Season with salt, pepper, and sugar.

The creamed chantarelles are often served as a main course with tiny new potatoes. The taste combination is fine and subtle. Chantarelles may also be served as a side dish with meats and roasts. This recipe can be used as a filling for an omelet.
Servings: 4.

CREAMED MORELLES [KORVASIENIMUHENNOS]

Morelles in Finland come out in the spring and are considered a great delicacy. Fresh ones are poisonous, but drying or cooking destroys the poison. Canned morelles are available in specialty shops.

1 cup canned morelles, drained
  (reserve liquid)
2 tablespoons butter
3 tablespoons unbleached white flour
1 cup liquid from the can

1 cup cream
1 teaspoon sea salt
  Pinch of raw sugar
⅛ teaspoon white pepper, or to taste

Chop the morelles. Melt the butter in a saucepan, add morelles, and cook 5 minutes. Sprinkle the mushrooms with flour, stir, and cook a few minutes. Let the flour become yellow, but not brown. Add the liquid little by little, stirring well after each addition. Add cream in the same way.

Simmer over low heat, half covered, 15 to 20 minutes. Season with salt, sugar, and pepper.

Serve like creamed chantarelles. Morelles are often served with reindeer and game dishes.
Servings: 4 to 6.

FRIED MUSHROOMS [PAISTETUT SIENET]

3½–4 cups chopped mushrooms   ⅛ teaspoon white pepper
    (preferably wild)   ¼ teaspoon chervil (optional)
  2–3 tablespoons butter   3 tablespoons sour cream
    1 medium onion, chopped   (optional)
    ½ teaspoon sea salt, or to taste

Put the chopped mushrooms into a heavy frying pan on low flame. They will release juice. Let them simmer in their own juice; the juice will gradually disappear.

Turn the heat on high, and add the butter and onion. Fry until onions and mushrooms are golden brown. Sprinkle with salt and pepper, and chervil, if wanted. Add sour cream, if you feel like it. Mushrooms have a delicate taste even without extras.

The best thing to accompany are potatoes boiled in their jackets and some tart preserve—lingonberry or black currant.
Servings: 4 to 6.

MUSHROOM SAUCE [SIENIKASTIKE]

1½–2 cups mushrooms, chopped fine   ¼ cup cream
    2 tablespoons butter   ½ teaspoon sea salt, or to taste
    2 tablespoons unbleached white   ⅛ teaspoon white pepper
      flour   Pinch of raw sugar
1½ cups beef, fish, or vegetable
    broth

Brown the mushrooms in butter. Sprinkle with the flour, stir, and cook a couple of minutes until the flour becomes light brown. Add the broth little by little, stirring and letting thicken after each addition. Add the cream and simmer 10 to 15 minutes, partially covered. Season with salt, pepper, and sugar.

Mushroom sauce is often served as a main course, with boiled potatoes. You may also use it as a sauce accompanying a fish or meat main course.
Servings: 4 to 6.

MUSHROOM BALLS [SIENIPULLAT]

    4 cups mushrooms   1 egg, lightly beaten
    1 onion, chopped fine   ½ teaspoon sea salt
    1 tablespoon oil or butter   ⅛ teaspoon white pepper
1/3 cup bread crumbs   Oil or butter
    ½ cup milk, or light cream

Drop the mushrooms into boiling water for about 2 minutes. Drain well and chop fine or put through a food mill. Brown the onion in oil or butter, add to the mushrooms. Soak the bread crumbs in milk or light cream, and combine with mushrooms. Add egg, salt, and pepper.

Using two spoons, form small balls and fry them like meatballs. Keep warm.

Serve as a main course as you would meatballs.
Servings: 4 to 6.

Chapter 9

VEGETABLE SIDE DISHES
[VIHANNEKSET]

Especially in the old days, there were very few kinds of fresh vegetables available in Finland. The vegetables grown had to adapt themselves to the short growing season and the sometimes chilly summer nights. But today many new vegetables are grown in hothouses, and many are imported.

The vegetables that grow in Finland—as any plants that grow in the northern parts of the world—have one great advantage: they are wonderfully strong in taste, much stronger than the same vegetables grown in the south. I have noticed this with almost all the vegetables I have tried, but especially with onions, tomatoes, and dill.

Hot Vegetables

Potato is still the most loved vegetable. Potatoes boiled in their jackets are usually served with everyday dinners. Before the potato became known, the small yellow turnip (close in taste and looks to the American white one) used to be almost the only vegetable used. It and the large yellow rutabaga are recommended instead of potato; they are much richer in vitamin C.

Probably the most original recipes are the Western Finland casseroles. Rutabaga, turnip, and cabbage are good and inexpensive vegetables in America, and these recipes give new ideas for their use.

NEW POTATOES [UUDET PERUNAT]

The real new potatoes are the first of the season: tiny, thumb-sized, with delicate jackets, and a sweet taste. In Finland they are often eaten as the main course flavored with dill and served hot.

Water to barely cover potatoes
1 tablespoon sea salt
1 bunch of dill stalks (reserve the leaves)

2 lbs tiny new potatoes
Dill leaves

Bring the salted water to a boil. Add the dill stalks and potatoes. Cover partially. Simmer until done: do not overcook. Pour away the water from the kettle and put the potatoes back on the heat, uncovered. Shake the kettle to let the potatoes dry well.

Serve the potatoes immediately from a warmed bowl which is lined and covered with a linen napkin to absorb any dampness. Sprinkle the potatoes with a lot of chopped dill leaves.

Serve with a dish that has a simple, pure taste: sugar-salted salmon (see page 22), salted or smoked fish, or smoked ham.
Servings: 4 to 6.

SMORGASBORD POTATOES [PERSILJAPERUNAT]

1½ lbs small potatoes (red or White Rose are good)
Water

2 teaspoons sea salt
1/3 cup chopped dill leaves
1/3 cup chopped parsley

Pick small, equal-sized potatoes. Peel them and make them nicely round. Steam them until done. If you don't have a steaming kettle, boil them in as little salted water as possible. Save the water for soups or breads!

Chop the dill and parsley very fine, and mix them together. Roll the potatoes in the herb mixture. Keep the potatoes hot in a bowl lined and covered with a napkin.

Serve to accompany smorgasbord fish dishes, or a smorgasbord plate (see page 15).
Servings: 4 to 6.

POTATO CASSEROLE [PERUNALAATIKKO]

2 lbs boiled potatoes
1 large onion, sliced
1½ tablespoons butter
¼ cup bread crumbs
2 eggs

2 cups milk or light cream
1 teaspoon sea salt
¼ teaspoon white pepper
¼ cup grated cheese

Peel and slice the boiled potatoes. Slice and brown the onion in ½ tablespoon of butter. Butter an ovenproof casserole or a 2-quart loaf pan with half of the remaining butter. Sprinkle it well with bread crumbs. Combine the casserole, alternating layers of potatoes and onions; the top layer will be potatoes.

Preheat the oven to 400°F. Beat the eggs lightly, add milk or cream, salt, and pepper. Mix well. Pour over the potatoes. Sprinkle the top with bread crumbs, grated cheese, and dot with the rest of the butter.

Bake about ½ hour. The top and sides should be dark brown and crisp.

Serve with simple fish or meat dishes, and add a colorful vegetable.
Servings: 4 to 6.

SWEETENED POTATO CASSEROLE
[HÄMÄLÄINEN PERUNATUUVINKI]

This is my favorite potato dish. The sweetening makes it different. It is from middle Finland, and used to be served with other casseroles on festival tables. It's also a Christmas dish.

2 lbs floury potatoes   2 cups milk
2 tablespoons butter   1 teaspoon sea salt
2 tablespoons unbleached white flour

Start making this the night before serving. Boil the potatoes in their jackets until done. Peel while still hot and mash them in a large bowl with butter. Add one tablespoon flour, mix well. Put the bowl into a warm place, cover, and let stand overnight. The potatoes will be sweetened by the flour.

The next morning, add 1 tablespoon flour, mix, and add the milk, then the salt. Preheat the oven to 300°F. Butter a 3-quart ovenproof glass dish and pour the mixture in. It should not fill the casserole more than 2/3 full; the potatoes will expand and bubble. Bake 3 hours. The casserole will have set, and the sides and top will have become brown and crusty.

Serve with meat dishes. It pays to make a larger portion. The casserole keeps well for about two weeks when refrigerated.
Servings: 6 to 8.

RUTABAGA CUBES [LANTTUKUUTIOT]

1 medium rutabaga   2 tablespoons blackstrap or regular
2 tablespoons butter, or a mixture of   molasses
    butter and oil   ¼ cup beef broth
½ teaspoon sea salt

Peel the rutabaga and cut into 1-inch cubes. In a heavy iron pot or a frying pan with a lid, brown the rutabaga in butter or butter and oil, until the cubes are browned on all sides.

Add the salt and molasses and lower the flame. Turn the rutabaga cubes so they are coated on all sides. Pour ¼ cup broth over, cover, and let hatch on very low flame until soft. Shake the pot once in a while and add broth if necessary.

Serve as you would potatoes, with pork or other meat dishes.
Servings: 4 to 6.

RUTABAGA CASSEROLE [LANTTULAATIKKO]

1 *lb rutabaga, peeled and cut into*
  pieces
2 *cups water*
1 *teaspoon sea salt*
½ *cup bread crumbs*
½ *cup milk*

1 *tablespoon blackstrap or regular*
  molasses
⅛ *teaspoon white pepper*
¼ *teaspoon nutmeg*
1 *egg*
1 *tablespoon butter or oil*

Cook the rutabaga pieces in salted water until soft. Meanwhile, soak all but 2 tablespoons of the bread crumbs in the milk. Preheat the oven to 350°F. Drain the rutabagas and reserve the liquid. Mash rutabagas, add the bread crumbs and milk, about 1 cup cooking liquid, molasses, pepper, nutmeg, and egg. Mix well.

Grease a 1-quart loaf pan or other oven casserole and sprinkle with 1 tablespoon bread crumbs. Pour the mixture in, sprinkle with the rest of the bread crumbs, and bake about 45 minutes.

Best with pork dishes. Serve also with other meat dishes.
Servings: 4 to 6.

SWEETENED RUTABAGA CASSEROLE [LANTTULOORA]

Originally an old Western Finland festival casserole, this used to be almost exclusively a Christmas dish. But now it's made commercially and sold all around the year. It is worth trying—rutabaga never tasted so good.

1 *lb rutabaga, peeled and cut into*
  pieces
½ *lb floury potatoes*
  Water for boiling
1/3 *cup unbleached white flour*
1 *cup milk*
½ *cup bread crumbs*
1/3 *cup cream*
1/3 *cup molasses or corn syrup*

¼ *cup (½ stick) butter, melted*
2 *eggs, lightly beaten*
1 *teaspoon sea salt*
¼ *teaspoon allspice*
⅛ *teaspoon white pepper*
⅛ *teaspoon nutmeg*
⅛ *teaspoon ginger*
  Butter

Start making this the night before serving. Boil the rutabaga pieces and potatoes separately in small amounts of water until done. When soft, drain and reserve the cooking liquids. Mash the rutabaga and potatoes together in a large bowl.

Add the flour and about ½ cup of the cooking liquid. Put into a warm place, cover, and let stand overnight to sweeten.

The next day, soak the bread crumbs in milk. Add them to the rutabaga-potato mixture. Add the cream, molasses or corn syrup, melted butter, eggs, salt, allspice, pepper, nutmeg, and ginger. Mix well.

Preheat the oven to 300°F. Grease a 2-quart loaf pan, and pour the mixture in. Flatten out the surface, and decorate with the back of a spoon by making rows of spoon-marks. Sprinkle with bread crumbs, and dot with a little butter. Bake 1½ to 2 hours. The surface should be golden brown, and the casserole will start coming loose from the sides of the dish.

Best with ham and pork dishes. Make a large amount and freeze.
Servings: 6 to 8.

WHITE TURNIP STEW [NAURISMUHENNOS]

1½ cups water	1 tablespoon butter
¼ teaspoon sea salt	1 tablespoon unbleached white flour
¼ teaspoon raw sugar or honey	¼ cup chopped fresh parsley
4 medium white turnips, or more if small, cut into cubes	

Bring the water to a boil, add salt and sugar. Throw in the turnips, cover, and simmer until they are soft, about 15 minutes. Drain and reserve the cooking liquid. Put the turnip cubes aside.

Melt the butter and cook the flour in it about 5 minutes, but do not brown. Pour in slowly about 1 cup cooking liquid, stirring well. Simmer and let thicken. Add the turnip cubes, cover, and simmer 2 minutes. Before serving, add parsley.

Serve with meat dishes.
Servings: 4.

WHITE TURNIP BAKE [NAURISPAISTOS]

1 lb small white turnips	2 tablespoons bread crumbs
1 cup water	1 egg
¼ cup ground almonds	¼ teaspoon sea salt
1 tablespoon molasses	1 teaspoon oil or butter

Cut the turnips into a few pieces. Boil them in water until soft. Drain, and reserve the liquid. Mash the turnips, and add the cooking liquid, ground almonds, molasses, bread crumbs, egg, and salt. Mix well.

Preheat the oven to 350°F. Grease a shallow ovenproof dish, and pour the mixture in. Bake about 30 minutes.

Serve with meat dishes.
Servings: 4.

STEWED CABBAGE [KAALIMUHENNOS]

1 lb white or red cabbage, chopped
   coarsely
1 cup water
1 tablespoon unbleached white flour
¼ cup cold water

¼ teaspoon sea salt, or to taste
1 tablespoon raw sugar or honey
1 tablespoon white or cider vinegar
2 tablespoons sweet or sour cream

Boil the cabbage in water until soft. Mix together the flour and cold water to make a smooth paste. Pour it slowly into the cabbage and water, stirring all the time. Simmer about 10 minutes. •

Remove from heat, and stir in salt, sugar or honey, vinegar, and cream.

Serve with meat dishes.
Servings: 4.

SAUERKRAUT CASSEROLE [HAPANKAALILAATIKKO]

   Butter or oil
3 tablespoons bread crumbs
2½–3 cups sauerkraut
2 eggs, lightly beaten

2 tablespoons melted butter
¾ cup sour cream
1 teaspoon raw sugar

Preheat the oven to 350°F. Grease well an oven casserole, and sprinkle with bread crumbs. Drain the sauerkraut and squeeze it dry.

In a bowl, combine the sauerkraut, lightly beaten eggs, melted butter, sour cream, and sugar. Mix well. Pour it into the casserole and sprinkle the top with bread crumbs. Bake 30 to 40 minutes.

Serve with simple meat dishes.
Servings: 4 to 6.

CARROT CASSEROLE [PORKKANALAATIKKO]

1 cup water
2/3 cup pearl barley, or brown rice
1–1½ cups milk
4–6 sweet carrots, grated
1 teaspoon sea salt

½ teaspoon raw sugar or honey
¼ teaspoon nutmeg
2 eggs, beaten
1 tablespoon butter
2–3 tablespoons bread crumbs

Bring the water to a boil, add the barley or rice, cover partially, and simmer until the water has been absorbed. Add 1 cup milk and simmer until it has been absorbed. If the barley is not yet done, add more milk—the barley should be done, but still firm, and there should be some milk left at the bottom of the pan. Cool a little.

Preheat the oven to 400°F. Mix the grated carrots, salt, sugar or honey, and nutmeg into the milk and barley or rice. Add the beaten eggs. Butter a 1½-quart oven casserole with half of the butter and sprinkle it with part of the bread crumbs. Pour the mixture in, sprinkle the surface with bread crumbs and dot with the rest of the butter. Bake about 40 minutes, or until the top and sides have browned nicely.

Serve with meat dishes. Especially good with veal dishes.
Servings: 4 to 6.

HATCHED BEETS [HAUDUTETUT PUNAJUURET]

1 lb raw beets, peeled and grated	1–2 tablespoons lemon juice
½ teaspoon sea salt	1 tablespoon grated horseradish
1 teaspoon raw sugar or honey	¼ teaspoon chervil (optional)

Put the grated beets into a thick-bottomed saucepan or in the top of a double boiler. Sprinkle with salt and sugar or honey, stir, cover, and let stand for ½ hour. Heat slowly, and let hatch over very low heat about ½ hour, or until soft. Keep tightly covered. Before serving, add the lemon juice, horseradish, and chervil.

Serve with meat and fish dishes. Very good with fish casseroles.
Servings: 4 to 6.

SPINACH CASSEROLE [PINAATTILAATIKKO]

1 cup pearl barley, or brown rice	1 teaspoon sea salt
1 cup water	2 teaspoons raw sugar or honey
1–1½ cups milk	2 eggs, beaten
1 lb spinach	1 tablespoon butter

Bring the water to a boil, add the barley or rice, and simmer, partly covered, until the water has been absorbed. Add 1 cup milk, simmer until it has been absorbed, and add more milk if necessary. The barley or rice should be done, but firm, and there should be some milk left at the bottom of the pan.

Preheat the oven to 400°F. Rinse the spinach well and put the leaves into a large kettle. Cover and steam until limp. Drain well and chop fine. Mix the barley or rice, spinach, salt, sugar or honey, and the beaten eggs. Grease a 2-quart oven casserole with half of the butter. Pour the mixture in, dot with the rest of the butter. Bake about 40 minutes.

Serve with meat and fish dishes. Especially good with salmon.
Servings: 4 to 6.

CREAMED SPINACH [PINAATTIMUHENNOS]

½ lb fresh spinach leaves	1 cup milk
1 tablespoon butter	½ teaspoon sea salt
2 tablespoons unbleached white flour	½ teaspoon raw sugar

Rinse the spinach leaves well, and put them into a kettle, but don't add water. Cover and steam until limp. Drain well and chop fine.

In a saucepan or in the top of a double boiler, melt the butter. Add the flour and cook, stirring, about 2 minutes. Add the milk little by little, stirring carefully and letting the mixture simmer and thicken after each addition. When all the milk has been added, simmer 5 minutes. Add spinach and simmer 5 more minutes. Remove from the heat and season with salt and sugar.

Serve with meat or fish courses. Especially good with salmon dishes; or as a filling for an omelet.
Servings: 4.

STEWED PEAS [HERNEMUHENNOS]

Traditionally served with Christmas ham, this dish is one of the old festival dishes.

1½ cups dry green peas
    Water
5–6 *cups water*

1 *tablespoon raw sugar*
½ *teaspoon sea salt, or to taste*
1 *tablespoon butter*

Soak the peas in water overnight or until they are soft and plump. Drain, and discard the soaking water.

Put the peas, about 4 cups water, and the sugar into a heavy-bottomed saucepan or the top of a double boiler. Bring to a boil, lower the heat to a minimum, cover, and simmer slowly 3 to 3½ hours. Every hour, check the water and add more if necessary. The stew will be ready when all the peas have broken, and let out their mushy insides. The stew will be rather thick, like a porridge.

Season with salt and butter.

Serve hot with ham and pork dishes.
Servings: 4 to 6.

BOILED PEA PODS [APPOSET]

A popular dish in the countryside, where the first and sweetest peas of the season are available.

1–1½ *lbs young, fresh, and plump*
    pea pods
2–3 *quarts water*

1–2 *tablespoons coarse sea salt*
1 *cup (2 sticks) melted butter*

Rinse the pea pods well. Bring the salted water to a boil, drop the pods in, and lower the heat. Simmer until the pods are done—when the thin skin on the top can be pulled off easily.

Drain the peas well and put the pods into a large ceramic bowl. Cover with a napkin.

Put the melted butter in the middle of the table. Take the pod in your fingers, dip it in butter, then suck the insides, discard the little stem and the hard veins on the sides, and reach for another.
Servings: 4 to 6.

STEWED KOHLRABI [KYSSÄKAALIMUHENNOS]

   1 *lb kohlrabi, leaves removed*
   1 *cup water*
   ½ *cup milk*
   1 *tablespoon unbleached white flour*

   1/3 *cup grated cheese, or to taste*
   ¼ *teaspoon sea salt*
   ¼ *teaspoon raw sugar or honey*

Peel and dice the kohlrabi. Boil the cubes in water until soft. Remove with a slotted spoon. Keep the liquid on the heat.

Combine the milk and flour into a smooth paste. Pour it slowly into the cooking liquid, stirring well all the time. Simmer about 10 minutes. Remove from heat, and add the grated cheese, kohlrabi cubes, salt, and sugar or honey.

Serve with plain meat dishes.
Servings: 4.

Salads

Fresh vegetables still aren't eaten in Finland as much as they are recommended, and the nutritionists are conducting a campaign to promote their use. The most popular salads are relatively simple, and great for everyday eating. Grated vegetables are especially refreshing, and quick to make. The most common kind of lettuce is Bibb, although lately iceberg and other varieties have been introduced.

OLD-FASHIONED SALAD [KERMANSEKAINEN SALAATTI]

   2 *small, fresh heads Bibb lettuce*

   ½ *European cucumber, cut into strips*

Dressing:
   1 *hard-boiled egg*
   1 *teaspoon prepared mustard*
   ½ *teaspoon sea salt*
   ½ *teaspoon raw sugar or honey*

   1 *tablespoon lemon juice or white vinegar*
   ½ *cup heavy cream, whipped*

Rinse the salad leaves well, and dry. Chill to crispen. Tear the leaves into pieces and put into a salad bowl with the cucumber strips.

To make the dressing, separate the hard-boiled yolk from the white. Mash the yolk with mustard, salt, and sugar or honey. Add lemon juice or vinegar, mix well. Fold in the whipped cream. Chill. Chop the egg white separately.

Pour the dressing over the salad just before serving. Sprinkle with chopped egg white.

Serve with meat or fish dishes.
Servings: 4 to 6.

CUCUMBER SALAD [KURKKUSALAATTI]

This is the simplest salad I know—and the best. Allow enough time for the marinade to seep through the cucumbers.

1 medium European cucumber, or
2 regular ones

3 tablespoons chopped fresh dill
leaves, or 1 tablespoon dried

Dressing:
½ cup white vinegar
¼ cup water

1 tablespoon raw sugar or honey
1 teaspoon sea salt

Wash the cucumber (do not peel the European one). Slice very thin. Put slices into a bowl, sprinkle dill between layers. Combine the ingredients for the dressing, letting the sugar or honey dissolve. Pour over the cucumbers. Cover the dish.

Chill the salad about 5 hours, or overnight. It is ready when the cucumber is limp and soaked through. Pour off some of the liquid before serving.

Serve with any dish that needs a touch of vinegary tartness.
Servings: 4 to 6.

RED CABBAGE SALAD [PUNAKAALISALAATTI]

1 small head of red cabbage, shredded
2 tablespoons chopped dill pickle

1 tablespoon grated onion
1 tart apple

Dressing:
2 tablespoons white or cider vinegar
2 tablespoons oil
1 teaspoon raw sugar or honey

½ teaspoon sea salt
½ teaspoon celery seed (optional)

Put the cabbage into a heavy, wide-bottomed bowl. With a heavy bottle or potato masher, pound the cabbage well, so that the cells break and the juice flows out. Add the chopped pickle and grated onion.

Combine the dressing ingredients, shake well, and pour over salad. Toss well, cover, and chill for at least 2 hours. Before serving, grate and add the apple.

Serve with any meat or fish dish.
Servings: 4 to 6.

CABBAGE-CRANBERRY SALAD [KAALI-KARPALOSALAATTI]

4 cups shredded white cabbage
2–3 carrots, coarsely grated

1 apple
¾ cup frozen cranberries

Dressing:
Juice of 1 grapefruit
1 teaspoon raw sugar or honey

¼ teaspoon ground marjoram
½ teaspoon ground aniseed

Pound the cabbage well in a wide-bottomed bowl with a heavy bottle or potato masher. Add the grated carrots and toss.

Combine the ingredients for the dressing. Pour over the salad and toss. Cover, and chill for at least 2 hours. Just before serving, grate and add the apple, and the still half-frozen cranberries.

Serve with meat dishes.
Servings: 6 to 8.

CARROT-APPLE SALAD [PORKKANA-OMENARAASTE]

1 cup grated carrots
1 cup grated apples

½ cup chopped fresh parsley

Dressing:
3 tablespoons lemon juice
1 tablespoon oil (optional)

1 teaspoon raw sugar or honey

Mix the carrots, apples, and parsley together.

Combine the dressing ingredients, and pour over the salad. Toss, and chill for ½ hour.

Serve with fish and meat dishes.
Servings: 4.

GRATED VEGETABLES [RAAKARAASTEVATI]

A decorative and light salad, which can also be served in the place of an appetizer.

1 cup grated carrots
1 cup grated rutabaga or white
   turnips

1 cup grated raw beets
1 cup grated apples
1 cup grated red or white cabbage

Dressing:
¼ cup lemon juice
½ cup orange juice
   oil to taste (optional)

¼ cup chopped parsley
¼ cup grated horseradish
½ cup sour cream

Make the salad as close to serving time as possible. Grate all the vegetables separately. Arrange the piles of grated vegetables on a large plate or tray. Mix the lemon and orange juice, oil, and parsley and sprinkle the vegetables with it.

In separate little cups in the middle of the tray, serve the horseradish and sour cream. Chill the tray before serving.

Serve as an appetizer or side salad. Let each person pick one or several kinds of vegetable, mix or eat them separately, and add horseradish or sour cream to taste.
Servings: 6 to 8.

GRATED RUTABAGA OR WHITE TURNIP
[LANTTU– TAI NAURISRAASTE]

This is a juicy and tasty fresh salad, one in the simple-but-good category.

2 cups grated rutabaga or white
turnips

½ cup finely chopped fresh parsley

Dressing:
¼ cup orange juice
1 tablespoon lemon juice

1 tablespoon oil (optional)
⅛ teaspoon white pepper

Mix the parsley and rutabaga or turnip.

Combine the dressing ingredients, and pour over the salad. Toss, cover, and chill for ½ hour.

Serve with meat dishes.
Servings: 4.

BEET SALAD [PUNAJUURISALAATTI]

4–6 medium beets, boiled in their
jackets
½ teaspoon sea salt, or to taste

1 tablespoon grated fresh
horseradish
2–3 tablespoons sour cream

Let the boiled beets cool. Peel and grate or cut into julienne strips. Sprinkle with salt, and toss. Mix the horseradish and sour cream, and pour into the salad. Toss.

Cover the bowl and chill at least overnight. The horseradish taste has to seep right through the beet strips.

Serve as a side dish for meats or fish. Nice with fish, meat, and mushroom casseroles.
Servings: 4 to 6.

MASHED CRANBERRIES [KARPALOSURVOS]

Instead of cooked lingonberry preserves, the fresh, mashed lingonberries are often served with meals. Make the same kind of fresh salad from cranberries.

1 lb fresh ripe cranberries

¼ cup raw sugar, or to taste

Put the cranberries into a deep bowl. With a heavy bottle or potato masher, mash the cranberries until most of them are broken. Stir in the sugar. The salad should be rather tart.

Chill well before serving.

Serve with meat and other dishes.
Servings: 6 to 8.

RADISHES WITH BUTTER [RETIISIT VOIN KANSSA]

My father taught me this way of eating radishes. It seems strange to many, but the butter cuts away some of the sharpness of the radishes and gives them a "round" taste.

2 bunches fresh, crisp, pretty radishes	2–3 tablespoons hard butter Salt

Wash and dry the radishes, and cut off the leaves and roots. Leave a little piece of stem. Cut the radishes into flowers, or just leave them as they are. Chill well.

With a wooden butter curler, make thin leaves of the butter, and arrange on a plate with crushed ice. Put the radishes around it, with a salt shaker.

Serve as a side vegetable or snack. Sprinkle the radish lightly with salt, add a tiny dot of butter on the top, and eat.
Servings: 4 to 6.

Pickles

The pickles chosen for this section are the ones that are most commonly used in Finland. The pickled beets especially can be had with almost any dish, but are most often served with the Baltic Herring. The recipe for homemade sauerkraut is really worth trying. Sauerkraut is real health food, and the homemade kind is much tastier than commercially prepared.

The quantities for the pickles are smaller than those usually given in the old-fashioned cookbooks. Few people have large cellars for keeping, or even a chance to make huge amounts of preserves. Multiply the quantities if you want larger portions.

PICKLED BEETS [ETIKKAPUNAJUURET]

1 lb beets, boiled

Marinade:

2 cups white vinegar	6 whole cloves
½ cup raw sugar	½ teaspoon white peppercorns

Slice the boiled beets and layer them in sterilized jars.

In a saucepan, combine the ingredients for the marinade, bring to a boil, cover, and simmer about 10 minutes. Let cool a little. Pour the marinade through a sieve over the beets. Cap the jars, and keep in a cold place a few days before serving.

Serve with meat and fish dishes. This is one of the most popular pickles in Finland.
Yield: 1 quart.

PICKLED ONIONS [HILLOSIPULIT]

1½ lbs small pearl onions   ¼ cup sea salt
2–3 cups water

Marinade:
2½ cups white vinegar   1 piece of ginger,
2/3 cup raw sugar   or ¼ teaspoon ground ginger
 ¼ teaspoon mace   10 whole white peppercorns

Peel the onions. Bring the salted water to a boil, and pour it over the onions. Let
stand 1 day, or overnight. Drain.

In a saucepan, combine the vinegar, sugar, mace, ginger, and peppercorns. Bring
to a boil, cover, and simmer 3 minutes. Drop in the onions, cover, and simmer
until the onions are half-done, transparent but still firm and crisp.

Sterilize small glass jars. With a slotted spoon, remove the onions from the marinade, and fill the jars about 2/3 full. Pour the marinade through a sieve over the
onions, to fill the jars. Cap the jars, let cool, and chill. Keep 4 to 5 days before
serving.
   Yield: 2 quarts.

DILL PICKLES [SUOLAKURKUT]

The best seasoning for these are the black currant leaves, which give a strong
taste and wonderful aroma. But if not available, use one of the other alternatives.

7–10 pickling cucumbers (enough to   5–7 dill crowns, or 1 teaspoon dill
   fill a 2-quart glass jar)   seeds
   1 tablespoon horseradish shavings   1 bunch dill stalks, leaves removed
   1 quart black currant, oak, or
   cherry leaves

Marinade:
   4 cups water   1 teaspoon whole white pepper-
   ½ cup white vinegar   corns
   ¼ cup coarse sea salt   1 garlic clove

Wash the cucumbers well, and wrap each in black currant or other leaves. Fit the whole cucumbers in the jar. Between them, put some horseradish shavings, and dill stalks and crowns, if used. Pour the cold marinade over the cucumbers. They should be covered totally. Keep the jar in a cold place 2 to 3 weeks before serving.

To make the marinade, in a saucepan, combine the water, vinegar, salt, peppercorns, garlic, and dill seed, if used. Bring to a boil, simmer a couple of minutes, and cool.

Serve with meat dishes or on sandwiches. These pickles keep 4 to 5 weeks after they are ready.
Yield: 2 quarts.

PICKLED MUSHROOMS I [ETIKKASIENET I]

1 quart small, cleaned mushrooms
2–3 cups water

2 teaspoons sea salt

Marinade:
3 cups wine vinegar
¾ cup raw sugar
1 teaspoon sea salt

2 teaspoons mustard seed
¼ teaspoon mace

Bring the salted water to a boil. Add the mushrooms, and let simmer until the mushrooms are shiny and firm, about 5 minutes. Drain well, and put the mushrooms into sterile glass jars, about 2/3 full.

Combine the marinade ingredients in saucepan, bring to a boil, cover, and simmer 10 minutes. Pour over the mushrooms through a sieve. Cap the jars, and keep in a cold place. Ready to serve in a few days.
Yield: 1½ quarts.

PICKLED MUSHROOMS II [ETIKKASIENET II]

1 quart small cleaned mushrooms
2–3 cups water

1 teaspoon sea salt

Marinade:
3 cups wine vinegar
1/3 cup raw sugar
1 teaspoon sea salt
½ tablespoon white peppercorns

¼ teaspoon mace
3 cloves
2 whole allspice
1 bay leaf

Bring the salted water to a boil, drop the mushrooms in, and simmer until they are shiny and firm, about 5 minutes. Drain, and let cool a little. Fill sterile glass jars with the mushrooms, about 2/3 full.

Combine the marinade ingredients in a saucepan, cover, bring to a boil, and simmer 10 minutes. Pour through a sieve over the mushrooms to fill the jars. Cap the jars, and keep in a cold place. Ready to serve in a few days.
Yield: 1½ quarts.

PICKLED GREEN TOMATOES [HILLOTUT TOMAATIT]

2 lbs small green tomatoes

Marinade:
2 cups white vinegar   *5 whole cloves*
1 cup raw sugar   *3 whole allspice*
¼ teaspoon mace   *1 bay leaf*

Rinse and dry the tomatoes, and prick all over with a needle. Combine the marinade ingredients in a saucepan, cover, bring to a boil, and simmer 10 minutes.

Add the tomatoes, lower the heat, cover, and simmer about 10 minutes, or until the tomatoes are soft, but still firm. Remove tomatoes with a slotted spoon and fill sterilized jars about 2/3 full. Pour the marinade over the tomatoes through a sieve. Cool a little, cap the jars, and keep in a cold place. Ready to serve in a couple of days.
    Yield: 2 quarts.

HOMEMADE SAUERKRAUT [HAPANKAALI]

It is fun—and basically very easy—to make your own sauerkraut and you can determine the degree of sourness you like.

4 lbs white, firm cabbage   *2 teaspoons coarse sea salt*

Pick white, firm, juicy heads of cabbage—winter cabbage is best. Dry, loose, young, green cabbage doesn't make good sauerkraut.

The cabbage is cut into long, thin strips which are sprinkled with coarse sea salt. The salt will draw water from the cabbage cells; you need liquid for the fermenting to take place. Too much salt prevents good fermenting. Use 1 teaspoon coarse salt for 2 pounds cabbage. Let stand ½ hour, or until some juice has come out.

Pounding is the most important step. Use a wooden potato masher or a heavy glass bottle. Put the cabbage into a large, heavy, wide-bottomed bowl. Mash and pound the cabbage so that the cells break and the juice flows out. Pound well; the cabbage must look transparent and be covered by juice.

For small portions, use large glass jars. The best jar is one in which the mouth narrows towards the top; it will help hold the cabbage down while the juice rises above it. For big portions, wooden barrels were used in the old days; the holes and splits were plastered with sour dough.

When packing the cabbage into the jar, it must be pressed down tightly. The jar is filled about 2/3 full. A weight is placed on top of the cabbage and the juice is allowed to rise above it, almost to the top of the jar. Cover with a clean cloth, fasten with a rubber band.

The jar must be kept in a warm place for the first few days, so that the fermenting process will start well and keep going. The pilot of a gas stove, covered with an asbestos plate, is fine for this. After 2 to 3 days the jar is moved to room temperature. You will actually see how the fermenting starts and the lactic acid is formed—there will be little bubbles escaping to the surface, and the liquid will turn milky and cloudy. Now the sauerkraut is well on its way.

Keep the kraut at room temperature 2 to 5 weeks, depending on the speed of the fermenting and on your individual taste. Tasting is the only thing that determines the readiness. When it's sour enough, cap, put it into the refrigerator, and the fermenting will stop. Good sauerkraut is transparent, golden yellow, and soft. It is rich in vitamins A, B, and C. The lactic acid is also good for your system.

Serve cold as a side vegetable. There are some sauerkraut-dish recipes in this book.
Yield: 2 quarts.

Chapter 10

DESSERTS
[JÄLKIRUUAT]

My favorite Finnish dessert is a hay straw strung with sweet, sunny-tasting wild strawberries and blueberries—like a string of red and blue beads. But wild strawberries can be enjoyed only by those who can pick them in the woods and fields—they do not take well to keeping, carrying, or preserving.

There is a great variety of other wild berries in Finland: raspberries, cranberries, and the most common of all, lingonberries. The two Arctic delicacies, cloudberry (*lakka* or *muurain*) and Arctic strawberry (*mesimarja*), are rare even in Finland; in America they can be bought in liqueur form. Gooseberries and black or red currants are the most common cultured garden berries in addition to strawberries and raspberries.

Most of the desserts in this book should not interfere with a sensible diet, if eaten in small quantities. The cold soups and puddings are relatively low in calories. It is a good idea to have desserts only on weekends and on special occasions so that they also become real treats and are enjoyed more.

Cold Soups and Puddings

These are quick, inexpensive, and light desserts and can be made of almost any fruits and berries that happen to be in season. The recipes in this section are the best known in Finland, but you can experiment with other fruits, berries, and juices. In Finland even the soups are served as desserts, but you may want to start a meal with one.

The soups and puddings are thickened with potato starch. It is available in many supermarkets and health food stores. Cornstarch may be used, but it is not as nice for these recipes.

Follow these rules carefully when thickening soups and puddings; and the result will be a pleasant, clear, and uniformly thickened dessert, instead of something that resembles heavy glue:

1) The potato starch is mixed with a little cold water before adding to the dessert. It dissolves easily, but separates again quickly. Stir it thoroughly just before using.

2) The liquid is usually heated until it is hot and about to reach the boiling point. If the fruits or berries are first cooked in the liquid, lift the pot off the heat before adding the thickening. If you pour the thickening into a liquid that's boiling hot, it will thicken too quickly, and become lumpy and gluey.

3) Pour the well-mixed potato starch into the hot liquid, slowly, stirring at the same time with a wire whisk. Do not whisk or beat: if you do, the pudding may turn sticky.

4) Put the dessert back on the heat, and bring to a quick boil. During this time the dessert will thicken, and turn from cloudy to clear. Do not let it simmer more than 1 minute. Then remove from the heat.

5) Pour the dessert into a bowl, and sprinkle the surface with sugar to prevent a scale from forming.

If your pudding is too thick, bring it to a boil again, and simmer a few minutes: it will loosen. If it is too thin, add more potato starch in the same way as before.

The quality of the potato starch may vary. But usually you need for soups, 1 to 2½ tablespoons potato starch for each quart of liquid. For puddings, you need 3 to 4 tablespoons per quart. Sour and acidic berries and fruits require more starch than sweet ones.

ROSE HIP SOUP [RUUSUNMARJAKEITTO]

4 cups water	2 tablespoons lemon juice
6 tablespoons dried rose hip powder	Slivered almonds
1½ tablespoons potato starch	Whipped cream
3 tablespoons raw sugar or honey	

Bring 3½ cups of the water to a boil. Stir in the rose hip powder, cover, lower the heat, and simmer 10 to 15 minutes. Pour the mixture through a very fine sieve, or a sieve lined with cheesecloth.

Mix the potato starch with ½ cup cold water, and pour it slowly into the rose hip mixture, stirring well with a wire whisk. Return to the heat, and simmer, stirring, until the soup thickens. Season with sugar or honey. Add lemon juice, and sprinkle the surface lightly with sugar. Cool.

Serve chilled, sprinkle with slivered almonds, and top with little clouds of whipped cream.

How to dry rose hips: Rose hips have more vitamin C than any other berry or fruit, and in addition, a good amount of B-vitamins, calcium, and iron. If you have roses, it pays to pick the hips and use them. Do not pick rose hips that grow right by a road; they may be full of lead.

Pick the rose hips when they are ripe and red, but not overripe. Remove the stems. Split the rose hips, and carefully remove from the inside all the seeds, the white parts, and the hairy substance.

Put the split hips on cookie sheets. Turn the oven on very low (less than 200°F), and dry the hips for 2 hours. After that, let them dry at room temperature.

Store the rose hips in air-tight containers or bags in a cool, dry place. Before using, soak in water: use the soaking water as well.

The dried hips can also be crushed or ground into powder.

Servings: 4 to 6.

APPLE SOUP [OMENAKEITTO]

4 cups water	1 tablespoon potato starch
¼ cup raw sugar or honey	¼ cup cold water
4 whole cloves	1 tablespoon lemon juice
1 stick cinnamon	2 tablespoons red berry juice
4–5 tart green apples, peeled, cored, and sliced	(optional: red juice gives a nice color)

Put the water, sugar or honey, and seasonings into a saucepan. Bring to a boil, cover, and simmer a couple of minutes. Add the sliced apples. Lower the heat, cover, and simmer gently until the apple slices are transparent, 10 to 15 minutes. Remove from the heat.

With a slotted spoon remove about half of the apple slices (the nicest ones) into a dessert bowl. Drain the rest, pressing all juice out. Discard the pulp. Mix potato starch and water, and pour into the juice, stirring well. Return to the heat, bring to a boil, and let thicken. Add lemon and berry juice. Pour over the apples.

Serve chilled as a dessert or a cold soup.

Servings: 4 to 6.

LEMON SOUP [SITRUUNAKEITTO]

4 cups water	3 tablespoons barley flour
¼ cup raisins	1/3 cup cold water
¼ cup raw sugar or honey, or to taste	Juice of 1–1½ lemons
1 cinnamon stick	1 tablespoon red berry juice

Bring the water, raisins, sugar or honey, and cinnamon to a boil. Cover and simmer 10 minutes. Remove from the heat.

Mix the barley flour and cold water into a smooth paste, and pour it slowly into the saucepan, stirring well with a wire whisk. Return to the heat, and simmer, stirring, about 10 minutes. Discard cinnamon stick.

When the soup has thickened, remove it from the heat. Add the lemon juice and the red berry juice. Pour into a dessert bowl, sprinke lightly with sugar, and cool.

Serve chilled as a dessert soup, with whipped cream or plain.
Servings: 4 to 6.

CRANBERRY SOUP [KARPALOKEITTO]

6 cups cranberry juice or drink, commercial or homemade
2/3 cup raw sugar or honey, if unsweetened juice is used

3 tablespoons potato starch
1/3 cup cold water

Combine the juice and sugar or honey in a saucepan. Mix together the cold water and potato starch. Heat the juice until almost boiling, then remove from the heat.

Slowly pour the potato-starch mixture into the juice, stirring well all the time with a wire whisk. Return to the heat and bring to the boiling point, stirring all the time. Simmer a minute or 2, until the soup thickens and becomes transparent. Remove from the heat. Pour into a dessert bowl, and sprinkle with sugar.

Serve chilled, as a dessert or cold appetizer soup. Add whipped cream, if desired.
Servings: 4 to 6.

CHERRY SOUP [KIRSIKKAKEITTO]

4 cups ripe, sweet cherries
3½ cups water
1 stick cinnamon
3 tablespoons raw sugar or honey, or less

1½ tablespoons potato starch
¼ cup cold water
2 tablespoons cherry wine (optional)
½ teaspoon grated orange peel

Clean the cherries and remove the pits. Bring the water to a boil, add the cherries and cinnamon stick, cover, and simmer until the cherries have lost color and rendered all juice, about 15 minutes. Drain through a sieve, pressing down on the cherries to get all the juice. Discard the cherry pulp. Put the juice back into the saucepan. Add sugar or honey.

Mix the potato starch and cold water into a smooth paste, and pour it slowly into the saucepan, stirring constantly with a wire whisk. Return it to the heat, and simmer, stirring, until the soup thickens and becomes transparent. Remove from heat. Season with cherry wine, if desired, and with orange peel. Sprinkle lightly with sugar and cool.

Serve chilled as a dessert or as an appetizer, with whipped cream or sour cream.
Servings: 4 to 6.

BLUEBERRY SOUP [MUSTIKKASOPPA]

2 pints blueberries
3 cups water
¼ cup raw sugar, or to taste

1½ tablespoons potato starch
¼ cup cold water

Put the cleaned blueberries and water into a saucepan, cover, and bring gently to a boil. Lower the heat, and simmer until the blueberries break and render juice, about 10 minutes. Try not to let boil. Season with sugar, and remove from heat.

Mix the potato starch and cold water, and pour slowly into the blueberries, stirring well. Return to the heat, bring to a quick boil, and remove. Pour into a dessert bowl, sprinkle with sugar, and cool.

Serve warm or chilled, with fresh pulla (see page 150). Sometimes I serve it poured over thin pancakes (see page 135). A real summer treat.
Servings: 4 to 6.

CRANBERRY PUDDING [KARPALOKIISSELI]

4 cups cranberry juice or drink
½ cup raw sugar or honey, or to taste, if unsweetened juice is used

¼ cup potato starch
1/3 cup cold water

Put the juice, and sugar, if used, into a saucepan, and heat, but do not let boil. Mix the potato starch with the cold water to make a smooth paste, and pour it slowly into the juice, stirring well with a wire whisk. Simmer until the pudding thickens and becomes transparent.

Remove from heat, sprinkle with sugar, and cool.
Another method: When fresh cranberries are used, bring 3 cups of cranberries and about 2 cups of water to a boil, lower the heat, and simmer until berries render juice. Drain, and discard pulp. Make as above, adding more water if necessary.

Serve chilled, with whipped cream seasoned with vanilla.
Servings: 4 to 6.

CARROT-CRANBERRY PUDDING
[PORKKANA-KARPALOKIISSELI]

1 recipe cranberry pudding
(see page 129)

1–1½ cups carrots, grated fine

Put the grated carrots at the bottom of a dessert bowl. Pour the hot cranberry pudding on top of them, and stir.

Sprinkle with sugar and cool.

Serve chilled, with whipped cream.
Servings: 4 to 6.

APPLE-CRANBERRY PUDDING
[OMENA-KARPALOKIISSELI]

3 cups cranberry juice or drink
1/3 cup raw sugar, if unsweetened
   juice is used
2 tart green apples, peeled, cored,
   and sliced

3½ tablespoons potato starch
1/3 cup cold water

Bring the cranberry juice, and sugar, if used, to a boil. Add the apple slices, lower the heat, cover, and simmer for about 10 minutes, or until the apples are transparent. Remove from heat. With a slotted spoon, transfer the apples into a dessert bowl.

Mix the potato starch and cold water into a smooth paste, pour it slowly into the cranberry juice, stirring well with a wire whisk. Simmer until the soup thickens and becomes transparent. Pour over the apple slices, stir, and sprinkle with sugar. Let cool.

Serve plain, or with whipped or light cream.
Servings: 4 to 6.

RED OR BLACK CURRANT PUDDING
[PUNA– TAI MUSTAVIINIMARJAKIISSELI]

4 cups red or black currant juice
   or drink
2/3 cup raw sugar, if unsweetened
   juice is used
3½ tablespoons potato starch
1/3 cup cold water

Heat the juice, and dissolve the sugar, if used. Heat only until warm. Mix the potato starch into the water, and pour it slowly into the juice, stirring well.

Heat the juice until it thickens and becomes clear. Try not to let the juice reach the boiling point; this way you will save more vitamin C. Pour into a dessert bowl, sprinkle with sugar, and cool.

Serve chilled, with fresh *pulla* (see page 150), or a spoonful of whipped cream.
Servings: 4 to 6.

GOOSEBERRY PUDDING [KARVIAISMARJAKIISSELI]

3–4 cups fresh, ripe gooseberries
2 cups water
1/3 cup raw sugar or honey, or to
   taste

2 tablespoons potato starch
1/3 cup cold water

Clean the gooseberries by pinching off the stems and the brown ends. Bring the water and sugar or honey to a boil. Add the gooseberries, lower the heat, and simmer, covered, until soft, about 15 minutes. Remove from the heat.

Mix together the potato starch and cold water, to make a smooth paste. Pour it slowly into the gooseberries, stirring well all the time. Simmer to thicken. Sprinkle with sugar and cool.

Serve chilled, plain or with cream.
Servings: 4 to 6.

RHUBARB PUDDING [RAPARPERIKIISSELI]

3 cups rhubarb, cut into ½-inch   ½ cup raw sugar or honey
   cubes   2 tablespoons potato starch
2½ cups water   ½ cup water

Scrape off the thin skin of the rhubarb stalks. Cut them in pieces. Bring the water and sugar or honey to a boil, add the rhubarb, cover, and simmer for about 15 minutes. Remove from the heat. Stir the rhubarb with a fork, so that it disintegrates into strings.

Mix the potato starch and cold water, to make a smooth paste. Pour it into the rhubarb mixture, stirring well. Return to the heat, and simmer until it thickens. Pour into a dessert bowl, sprinkle with sugar, and cool.

Serve with heavy cream.
Leftover pudding: Use for Stablemaster's Pudding (see page 142).
Servings: 4 to 6.

RASPBERRY PUDDING [VAAPUKKAKIISSELI]

2 pints fresh raspberries   3 tablespoons potato starch
2½ cups water   1/3 cup cold water
1/3 cup raw sugar or honey

Put half of the raspberries in a dessert bowl. Bring the water and sugar or honey to a boil, and to it add the rest of the raspberries. Cover, bring to a boil, and simmer until the berries render all juice. Drain the juice, pressing down on the berries, and discard the pulp.

Mix the potato starch and cold water to make a smooth paste, and pour it slowly into the raspberry juice, stirring well. Return to the heat, and simmer until the pudding thickens and becomes transparent. Pour it over the raspberries in the dessert bowl, stir. Sprinkle with sugar and cool.

Another method: If you use frozen, sugared berries, use 2 packages raspberries, 2 cups water, and no extra sugar. Pick the prettiest berries to use whole.

Serve chilled, with whipped cream flavored with vanilla.
Servings: 4 to 6.

STRAWBERRY PUDDING [MANSIKKAKIISSELI]

2 pints ripe, sweet, small strawberries
1½ cups water

2–3 tablespoons raw sugar or honey
2 tablespoons potato starch
½ cup cold water

Clean the strawberries. Pick the ripest and prettiest—about half of the berries—and put them into a dessert bowl. Put the other half into a saucepan, and pour the water over. Bring to a boil, cover, and simmer 10 minutes, or until the berries have rendered juice. Drain, and discard the pulp. Put the juice back into the saucepan and season with sugar or honey.

Mix the potato starch and cold water into a smooth paste, and pour slowly into the juice, stirring well. Put the pan back on the heat, and simmer until the pudding thickens and becomes transparent. Pour over the whole strawberries and stir. Sprinkle with sugar and cool.

Serve chilled, plain or with whipped cream.
Servings: 4.

PRUNE PUDDING [LUUMUKIISSELI]

Prune Pudding is a traditional Christmas dessert.

2 cups pitted prunes
3 cups water or prune juice
1 stick of cinnamon

2 tablespoons potato starch
½ cup cold water
1 tablespoon Madeira wine

Soak the prunes in water or prune juice, until plump. Add the cinnamon stick. Put the prunes and liquid into a saucepan, bring to a boil, lower the heat, cover, and simmer until the prunes are soft and ready to break. Transfer the prunes with a slotted spoon into a dessert bowl. Remove the cinnamon stick.

Mix the potato starch and cold water to a smooth paste, and pour it slowly into the liquid, stirring well. Simmer until it thickens and becomes transparent. Season with Madeira. Pour over the prunes, stir, and sprinkle with sugar. Let cool.

Serve chilled with whipped cream.
Servings: 4 to 6.

FRUIT PUDDING [SEKAHEDELMÄKIISSELI]

8 oz package mixed dried fruit
4 cups water, or unsweetened
  apricot or apple juice
1 stick of cinnamon

3 tablespoons raw sugar or honey
2½ tablespoons potato starch
¼ cup cold water

Soak the fruit in the water or juice a couple of hours, or until plump. Put the fruit, water or juice, and cinnamon into a saucepan. Cover, bring to a boil, and simmer until the fruit is soft, about 15 minutes. With a slotted spoon, remove the fruit to a dessert bowl.

Remove the liquid from the heat. Add sugar or honey, stir. Mix potato starch and cold water to a smooth paste, and pour slowly into the liquid, stirring well. Return to the heat, and simmer until it thickens and becomes transparent. Pour over the fruit, stir. Sprinkle with sugar and cool.
  Another method: Use only dried apricots.

Serve chilled, with milk or light cream.
Servings: 6 to 8.

WHIPPED PORRIDGE [VISPIPUURO]

4 cups cranberry juice
½ cup raw sugar, if unsweetened
  juice is used

¾ cup farina (preferably not the
  precooked kind)

Heat the juice and sugar, if used, add farina, and cook according to instructions on the farina package.

Pour the porridge into a mixing bowl. With an electric or rotary beater, beat the porridge until it becomes pink, light, and airy. Pour the fluffy porridge into dessert bowls and chill.

Serve for dessert, with light cream.
Servings: 4 to 6.

TAPIOCA PUDDING [HELMIRYYNIKIISSELI]

1 cup tapioca
2 cups milk
1 tablespoon butter
2 tablespoons raw sugar

1/3 cup ground almonds
  Grated peel and juice of 2 lemons
¼ cup raisins, soaked until plump
3 eggs

Soak the tapioca in cold water a few hours or overnight. Drain, discard soaking water. Cook the tapioca in milk until soft. Add the butter, and cool.

Preheat the oven to 375°F. Add the sugar, almonds, lemon juice and peel, and raisins to the tapioca. Beat the eggs well, and add to tapioca. Butter an ovenproof casserole, and pour the mixture in. Bake 30 to 45 minutes. Cool.

Serve warm or cold. Add a dessert sauce, if you want.
Servings: 4 to 6.

MILK PUDDING [MAITOKIISSELI]

¼ cup raw sugar
2½ cups milk
¼ cup cornstarch or potato starch

1 egg
½ teaspoon vanilla extract, or to
taste

Combine the sugar and 1½ cups of the milk, in a heavy-bottomed saucepan, or in the top of a double boiler. Bring to a boil. Lower the heat.

Mix together the cornstarch or potato starch and 1 cup of milk, to make a smooth paste. Pour it slowly into the milk and sugar, stirring with a wire whisk. Bring to a boil again, and let simmer about 10 minutes, or until it thickens and the floury taste disappears. Stir now and then, to prevent clotting.

Beat the egg. Remove the pudding from the heat, pour ¼ cup of the hot pudding into the egg, stir, and then stir the egg mixture into the pudding, beating until smooth and silky. Add vanilla. Let cool.

Serve chilled, with a spoonful of jam—strawberry is the favorite.
Servings: 4.

STUDENTS [YLIOPPILAAT]

The dessert is named after the white hats worn by students in Finland. This dessert needs a cold sauce to accompany it.

1½ cups milk
½ cup farina
¼ cup ground almonds
¼ cup raisins

Grated peel of half a lemon
¼ teaspoon sea salt
¼ cup raw sugar
¼ teaspoon vanilla extract

Bring the milk to a boil, add the farina. Cover, and simmer until the farina becomes thick like a porridge. Add the almonds, raisins, lemon peel, salt, sugar, and vanilla. Let cool a little.

Rinse small, round-bottomed cups with cold water, to be used as molds. Fill them with the mixture, pressing down tightly. Fill about 2/3 full. Let cool in cups, and chill. Before serving, turn the little puddings onto a serving plate. Pour sauce over them.

Serve the students with any of the dessert sauces (see page 143) or cold soups.
Servings: 4 to 6.

Other Desserts

The best-loved desserts are the pancakes, which are a special favorite of children. Some of these desserts are old, traditional favorites, but there are also a few new ones.

THIN PANCAKES [LETUT]

1 egg
1 teaspoon sea salt
1½ teaspoons raw sugar
1½ cups milk, or 1 cup buttermilk
   and ½ cup water

1 tablespoon oil or melted butter
1¼ cups unbleached white flour
Butter or oil

Beat the egg lightly, add salt and sugar. Pour in the milk, or buttermilk and water. Whisk in the flour, and beat well to make a thin, smooth batter. Add oil or melted butter. Let the batter stand in a warm place 1 to 2 hours. It will thicken.

Usually the pancakes are fried in a pancake pan with small separate rings, but they can also be made in a crêpe pan. Fry the pancakes in a very hot pan, greasing the pan before making each pancake. Try to make them brown and crisp at the edges.

Serve as a dessert, right from the pan. Sprinkle with sugar, or serve with strawberry or other preserves. Or mash fresh strawberries and sugar, and serve on top of the pancakes.

Servings: 4.

CREAM PANCAKE [KERMAPANNUKAKKU]

1 teaspoon butter or oil
2 eggs
¼ cup raw sugar

¾ cup heavy cream, whipped
½ cup unbleached white pastry flour
¼ teaspoon sea salt

Preheat the oven to 350°F. Grease a 9-inch glass cake pan. Beat the eggs and sugar until thick and foamy. Fold the whipped cream into eggs. Sift in the flour, stirring quickly. Add salt. Pour the mixture immediately into the cake pan.

Bake 30 to 40 minutes. Take out and let cool in a draftless place.

Serve as a dessert, spread with good jam. The taste is rich and satisfying. You may also serve it as a cake, with coffee. Good also sprinkled with lemon or orange juice.

Servings: 4 to 6.

OVEN PANCAKE [UUNIPANNUKAKKU]

Oven pancake is traditionally a Thursday dish, to follow the pea soup main course.

4 eggs
2 tablespoons raw sugar
1 cup milk

1 teaspoon sea salt
2/3 cup gluten flour
2/3 cup unbleached white flour

Preheat the oven to 425°F. Beat the eggs and sugar well, until thick and foamy. Add the milk and salt. Stir in the gluten flour, and beat well. The idea is to give the batter a firm structure so it can rise in the oven. Stir in the unbleached flour, and keep beating about 10 minutes.

Grease well a 2-inch deep oven pan. Pour the batter into the pan, and put in the oven immediately. Bake 20 to 25 minutes. The pancake will bubble and parts of it will rise; the top and sides should be brown, the insides still a little chewy.

Serve warm or cold, with strawberry preserves.
Servings: 4 to 6.

SHROVE TUESDAY BUNS [LASKIAISPULLAT]

For this dessert, make the round *pullas* a little larger than usual. Buns are served traditionally on Shrove Tuesday.

6 large pullas (see page 150)

Filling:
3–4 oz almonds, blanched and ground
    fine
½ cup confectioners' sugar

1 tablespoon hot water
1 teaspoon cognac

Topping:
½ cup cream, whipped

Cut a lid off the top of each bun. Scoop out some of the insides of the bun.

Combine the ingredients for the filling into a thick paste. Fill the buns with this mixture. Whip the cream until thick. Put a spoonful of whipped cream on top of the filling, and cover loosely with the lid.

Serve as a dessert with coffee or milk.
Servings: 6.

PASHA

Every Russian emigrant family in Finland swears in the name of their best, one and only real pasha recipe. This is one of them. The original, large recipe feeds a whole large family or party; I have made the small recipe for 6 to 8 servings. It is also less sweet.

Original large recipe:

1 lb butter	1 lb raw sugar
1 whole egg	1 cup ground almonds (optional)
3 egg yolks	½ cup candied orange peel (optional)
3 lbs homemade curd from 9 quarts	1 cup raisins (optional)
buttermilk (see page 188)	2 tablespoons vanilla extract
1½ lbs sour cream	

Small recipe:

¼ lb butter	½ cup raw sugar
1 egg	¼ cup ground almonds
1 lb curd from 3 quarts buttermilk	2 tablespoons candied orange peel
(see page 188)	¼ cup raisins
1 cup sour cream	½ teaspoon vanilla extract

In a heavy, large kettle or in a double boiler, melt the butter. Beat the eggs lightly. Add the curd to the butter, forcing it through a sieve. Add the eggs, sour cream, sugar, almonds, orange peel, and raisins. Mix well.

Heat the mixture slowly, stirring all the time. Bring it to the boiling point, but do not let it actually boil. When the mixture is heated, it will become thinner. Just before the boiling point, remove from the heat.

Put the kettle into a bowl of cold water, and let cool while stirring. It will thicken again. When somewhat cooled, add the vanilla.

Line an unglazed earthenware flowerpot with a double thickness of wet cheesecloth, leaving some cloth hanging over the edges. Pour the pasha mixture into the pot, and put the pot into a bowl. Press down the pasha, and tie the cheesecloth over it. Put a weight on the pasha.

Let the pasha stand in a cool place 2 to 3 days. The excess liquid will drip into the bowl and seep through the walls of the flowerpot. I find it best to let it stand at least 3 days. Before serving, turn the pasha onto a plate, and remove the cheesecloth.

Serve as a dessert. A thin slice is enough per serving. Decorate the pasha with orange slices if you want. Sometimes I serve it with my American creation, a kumquat sauce which I make from ripe kumquats, water, and eucalyptus honey by simmering the mixture until it becomes syrupy, then draining away the peels. But ordinarily pasha is served plain.

Servings: Original recipe: 20 or more.
Small recipe: 6 to 8.

UNCOOKED PASHA [KEITTÄMÄTÖN PASHA]

This old recipe is from the Karelian town Terijoki, now the Russian Zelenogorsk. In the original wooden pasha forms, there are always the Cyrillic letters XB, meaning "Christ has risen."

1 lb curd from 3 quarts buttermilk	1/3 cup melted butter
(see page 188)	¼ cup raw sugar
2 eggs	¼ cup raisins
1/3 cup sour cream	½ teaspoon vanilla extract

Press the curd through a sieve into a bowl. Add the eggs one by one, beating after each addition. Add the sour cream, stirring well, then the melted butter. Beat until the mixture is creamy, smooth, and light. Add the sugar, raisins, and vanilla.

Line an unglazed earthenware flowerpot with a double thickness of wet cheesecloth. Pour the mixture in. Press down, and tie the cheesecloth over the pasha. Put the pot into a bowl, and set a weight on top of the pasha. Let stand in a cool place 2 days.

Servings: 8 to 10.

BUTTERMILK FOAM [PIIMÄVAAHTO]

2 eggs, separated	1 cup water
¼ cup raw sugar	2 cups buttermilk
2 envelopes unflavored gelatin	Juice of 1 lemon

Beat the eggs yolks and sugar until lemon-colored. Sprinkle the gelatin over cold water to soften, and heat to dissolve. Add the buttermilk to the eggs and sugar, then fold in the lemon juice, and gelatin mixture. Put in a cold place until it starts to thicken.

Beat the egg whites until stiff. When the gelatin has started to thicken, and will hold the foam, fold in the egg whites, mixing quickly. Pour the foam into a dessert bowl, and chill to set.

Spoon into individual dessert bowls, top with some dessert sauce if desired.
Servings: 4 to 6.

MÄMMI

This is the original Finnish Easter dessert, made of rye flour and rye malt by the method of sweetening. When I was a child it was still sold in baskets made of birch bark. The Finns believe that it's impossible for a foreigner to appreciate *mämmi*, but I quite disagree—the problem is finding the needed rye malt for the sweetening.

2½ quarts water (10 cups)	½ lb rye malt, finely ground
1 lb rye flour	¼ cup ground orange peel

Heat 4 cups water until it bubbles. Whisk in a quarter of the rye flour and a quarter of the malt. Remove from the heat and put the kettle in a warm place. The pilot of a gas stove is fine. The kettle should never be allowed to cool off, but it shouldn't ever boil, either. On the top of the mixture, sprinkle a rather thick layer of rye flour. Cover with a towel, and let stand for 1 hour. The sweetening will start.

Heat 2 cups water until bubbles break to the surface. Pour it into the mixture in the kettle, and stir. On the top, sprinkle a thick layer of rye flour (1/3 of what is left), and rye malt (1/3 of what is left). Cover with the towel, and let stand 1 more hour.

Heat 2 cups water until bubbles break to the surface, add another 1/3 of the rye flour and of the rye malt.

Now heat the last 2 cups water, this time until it actually boils, and pour in. Sprinkle the rest of the rye flour and malt over the kettle, cover, and let stand 1 more hour.

Now the *mämmi* should have the thickness of porridge. Add the ground orange peel, and if necessary to make the mämmi thicker, a little more rye flour. Simmer uncovered about 30 minutes, stirring regularly. Remove from the heat, and beat until it is completely cooled off.

Preheat the oven to 350°F. Butter a shallow oven casserole, and pour the mixture into it. Bake about 3 hours, or until done. The ready *mämmi* has a sticky texture. When done, brush the surface with a mixture of sugar and water. Cool.

Serve cold, scooped into small dessert bowls. Sprinkle with sugar and pour heavy cream over it. It is a heavy dish, so serve small portions. If covered this dish will last for at least 3 weeks.

ULLA'S CURD JELLY [RAHKAHYYTELÖ]

¾ lb curd, made of 2 quarts
    buttermilk (see page 188)
1-2/3 cups light cream
¼ cup raw sugar or honey
    Grated peel of ½ lemon

1 teaspoon grated orange peel
½ teaspoon ground cardamom
2 drops almond extract
1 envelope unflavored gelatin
1/3 cup cold water

Press the curd through a sieve into a bowl. Add the light cream, and sugar or honey, lemon peel, orange peel, cardamom, and almond extract.

Soften the gelatin in cold water, and heat to dissolve. Pour the gelatin into the curd mixture and stir. Pour into a mold that's been rinsed with cold water. Chill until set. Unmold onto a serving platter.

Slice pieces as from a cake. Serve with orange sauce (see page 144), or lemon sauce (see page 144).

BAKED APPLES [UUNIOMENAT]

Use the greenest, tartest apples you can find: cooking apples are the best.

4 large tart apples　　　　　　　　　　*½ teaspoon cinnamon*
2 tablespoons molasses or honey　　　*¼ cup water*
2 tablespoons ground almonds

Preheat the oven to 425°F. Rinse, dry, and core the apples. Put them into a heavy oven pan. Mix together the molasses or honey, almonds, and cinnamon. Fill the centers of the apples with this mixture. Pour the water into the bottom of the pan.

Bake in oven until crisp and brown on the outside, soft on the inside. It's difficult to tell exact baking time, as apples vary. Check often, and brush the apples with the liquid that forms on the bottom of the pan.

Serve warm, plain or with cold vanilla sauce (see page 145).
Servings: 4.

WHIPPED CRANBERRY JELLY [VATKATTU KARPALOHYYTELÖ]

1 envelope gelatin　　　　　　　　　　*¼ cup honey, if unsweetened juice*
½ cup cold water　　　　　　　　　　　　*is used*
　　　　　　　　　　　　　　　　　　　　　1½ cups cranberry juice

Soften the gelatin in cold water, and heat to dissolve. Add the honey if used, and dissolve. Pour the gelatin mixture into the cranberry juice, and stir.

Chill until almost set. Beat with an electric beater until pink and foamy. Chill to set. The foaminess should stay while the dessert chills.

Decorate with a spoonful of whipped cream, and a few candied cranberries (see page 141) if you have any.
Servings: 6 to 8.

ORANGE RICE [APPELSIINIRIISI]

1 cup rice　　　　　　　　　　　　　　　*1 cup heavy cream*
3–4 juicy oranges　　　　　　　　　　　*½ teaspoon grated orange peel*
¼ cup raw sugar　　　　　　　　　　　　*¼ teaspoon vanilla extract*

Boil the rice in water until soft, but still firm and loose. Drain well, and cool. Chill.

Peel the oranges; carefully remove the white parts. Separate into wedges, and cut the wedges into 2 or 3 pieces. Put the oranges into a bowl with the sugar. Toss well, and let stand 15 minutes. Chill.

Just before serving, whip the cream, season with orange peel and vanilla. Combine the rice, oranges, and whipped cream, toss, and pour into a chilled dessert bowl.

Spoon into individual dessert bowls.
Servings: 4 to 6.

CANDIED CRANBERRIES [SOKEROIDUT KARPALOT]

When commercial candies weren't available, this sugary-tart candy was the favorite of all kids.

2 cups fresh ripe cranberries   *½ cup confectioners' sugar*
2 egg whites

Freeze the cranberries, uncovered, for about 15 minutes. This will make them a little frost-bitten, which does them good.

Beat the egg whites lightly, and pour into a shallow bowl. Put the sugar on a plate. Dip the cranberries, one by one, in the egg whites, and then roll, with light fingers, in the sugar, until well coated. Put the berries on a foil-covered cookie sheet.

Preheat the oven to 200°F. Dry the berries slowly in the oven, leaving the door open, for about 1½ hours, until the egg and sugar form a firm coating. Cool.

Serve as candy, or use to decorate desserts.

Leftover Desserts

Save your leftover breads, cakes, and cookies for these simple, old-fashioned desserts. Have these desserts with a light meal that doesn't include many other flour and bread products.

POOR KNIGHTS [KÖYHÄT RITARIT]

Similar to French toast, the Knights are served as a dessert in Finland.

1 egg, beaten   *6 slices of dried leftover white bread*
½ cup milk   *or pulla (see page 150)*
⅛ teaspoon sea salt   *2 tablespoons butter*
1 tablespoon unbleached white flour

Beat the egg, and mix with milk, salt, and flour. Soak the bread slices in the mixture until they are soaked through. Fry them in butter on both sides until dark brown. Keep warm until serving.

May be served plain, but often they are decorated with a spoonful of lingonberry or cranberry preserves and vanilla-flavored whipped cream.
Servings: 6.

PARSON'S TRIFLE [PAPPILAN HÄTÄVARA]

This dessert got its name because it's an easy dessert to prepare, for surprise guests, which in a parsonage you always have.

1 cup heavy cream
2 tablespoons raw sugar
2–3 cups leftover cookies, rusks, and cake pieces

2 cups sweetened cranberry juice
1 cup lingonberry, cranberry, or other preserves

Whip the cream and sugar. Dip the cookie, rusk, and cake pieces in the juice, until soaked but still firm.

Arrange the dessert in a decorative glass bowl: start with a layer of cookies, top with preserves, and cover with whipped cream. Repeat if necessary. Chill.
Servings: 4 to 6.

SOUR BREAD PUDDING [HAPANLEIPÄVANUKAS]

2 cups sour bread crumbs
2 tablespoons butter
½ teaspoon cinnamon
1/3 cup raw sugar

1 cup apple sauce
½ cup ordinary bread crumbs
2 eggs, lightly beaten
1 tablespoon butter, for greasing

Fry the sour bread crumbs in butter, add cinnamon and raw sugar. Cool. To make the apple sauce mixture, combine the apple sauce, the ordinary bread crumbs, and the eggs, and mix well.

Preheat the oven to 400°F. Grease an oven casserole with half of the butter. On the bottom, spoon half of the sour bread crumbs. On top of it, spread the apple sauce mixture. Top it with the rest of the sour bread crumbs. Dot with the rest of the butter. Bake 30 to 45 minutes.

Serve warm, with whipped cream or cold vanilla sauce (see page 145).
Servings: 4 to 6.

STABLEMASTER'S PUDDING [TALLIMESTARIN KIISSELI]

1½ cups bread crumbs, preferably sour bread crumbs
1½ tablespoons cocoa powder
1 tablespoon raw sugar

¼ teaspoon vanilla extract
1 recipe rhubarb pudding (see page 131), or gooseberry pudding (see page 130)

Heat a heavy frying pan. Roast the sour bread crumbs mixed with cocoa, until they become dry and brown, but do not burn. Remove from the pan, add sugar and vanilla, and cool.

Fill individual dessert bowls first with a layer of the rhubarb or gooseberry pudding, then 2 or 3 tablespoons of the crunchy bread crumb mixture. Top with rhubarb or gooseberry pudding. Serve before the crumbs get soaked.

Serve plain or with light cream.
Servings: 4 to 6.

GRANDMA'S BREAD PUDDING [MUMMON LEIPÄVANUKAS]

Grandma loved this dessert and made sure there were always sour bread slices in the pudding. Make this with tenderness: it's a recipe you perfect with practice.

Leftover sour rye bread, other
bread, and pulla *slices*
(see page 150)
3–4 *cups sweetened cranberry*
juice
2 *tablespoons butter*

1 *cup lingonberry or cranberry*
preserves, or mashed cranberries
seasoned with sugar (see
page 116)
1 *tablespoon raw sugar*

Preheat the oven to 425°F. Soak the bread slices in the juice until completely saturated. Butter a 2-quart glass casserole or loaf pan with half of the butter.

Combine the pudding in layers. First a layer of soaked bread slices, and then preserves or crushed berries. Repeat. The top layer will be bread, dotted with the rest of the butter and sprinkled with sugar. Pour the remaining soaking juice over the pudding. Bake 30 to 45 minutes. The top and sides of the pudding should be crisp and brown, but the insides should still be moist and juicy.

Serve either warm or cold, plain or with cold milk poured over.
Servings: 4 to 6.

Dessert Sauces

Use these everyday versions as substitutes for rich egg-yolk-and-cream-thickened sweet sauces. Top all kinds of puddings, pancakes, and jellies.

STRAWBERRY SAUCE [MANSIKKAKASTIKE]

1 *pint ripe, sweet strawberries*   1 *tablespoon raw sugar or honey*

Clean the strawberries and put them in a blender with the sugar or honey. Blend until liquid. Pour into a pitcher, and chill.

Serve on puddings and pancakes.
Servings: 4 to 6.

RASPBERRY SAUCE [VADELMAKASTIKE]

1 pint raspberries   *1 tablespoon raw sugar or honey*

Blend half of the raspberries and sugar or honey in blender until liquid. If there are still some seeds left, put the sauce through a sieve.

Combine the other half of the whole raspberries with the sauce. Chill.

Serve with Buttermilk Foam (see page 138), or with puddings.
Servings: 4 to 6.

LEMON SAUCE [SITRUUNAKASTIKE]

1 egg yolk   *1 teaspoon potato starch*
2–3 tablespoons honey   *1 cup water*
Juice and grated peel of 1 large
lemon

In the top of a double boiler, beat together the egg yolk and honey, add lemon juice and grated peel. Add potato starch mixed with the water.

Heat, whisking all the time, until the mixture thickens and becomes quite transparent. Remove from the heat, and beat until cooled. Chill.

Serve on curd jelly (see page 139), students (see page 134), or puddings.
Servings: 4 to 6.

ORANGE SAUCE [APPELSIINIKASTIKE]

3 cups orange juice (4–5 oranges   *2 tablespoons potato starch*
squeezed)   *1 tablespoon red berry juice*
Grated peel of 2 oranges   *Few drops of orange-flavored liqueur*
2 tablespoons raw sugar or honey   *(optional)*

Use a double boiler for cooking. In the top of the double boiler, combine the orange juice, orange peel, sugar or honey, and potato starch. Whisk well. Heat, whisking all the time, until the sauce thickens.

Color it with the red berry juice, and flavor with orange liqueur, if desired. Cool.

Serve chilled with puddings, jellies, and pancakes.
Servings: 4 to 6.

WINE SAUCE [VIINIKASTIKE]

1 cup water   *1/3 cup raw sugar or honey*
1 cup white wine   *1½ teaspoons potato starch*
¼ cup Madeira or sherry
Grated peel and juice of 1
lemon

Use a double boiler. Combine the water, wines, lemon juice and peel, sugar or honey, and potato starch. Whisk well. Heat slowly, whisking all the time, until the sauce thickens.

Let cool, whisking all the time. Chill.

Serve on puddings.
Servings: 4 to 6.

VANILLA SAUCE [VANILJAKASTIKE]

2½ cups milk
3 tablespoons raw sugar
1 tablespoon cornstarch or potato starch

2 egg yolks
½ teaspoon vanilla extract

Use a double boiler. Whisk together all the ingredients. Heat, whisking all the time, until the mixture thickens.

Remove from heat, and beat until the sauce cools. Chill.

Another method: This is an everyday version of the sauce. For a special sauce, use 4 or 5 egg yolks, cream instead of milk, and omit the cornstarch or potato starch. This version has far more calories.

Serve on baked apples (see page 140), apple pies, and tarts.
Servings: 6 to 8.

Chapter 11

BAKING
[LEIVONNAISET]

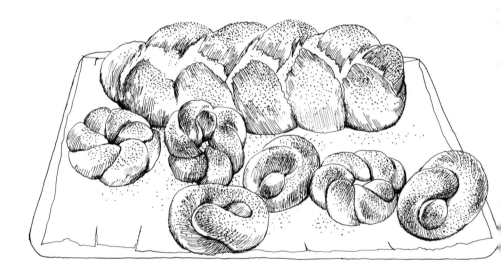

The Finnish breads rely mostly on the flavors of the grains. They aren't ever as heavy as the American nut and fruit type breads, but compared to the fluffy white commercial breads, Finnish breads are solid and substantial, and they taste like real bread.

Finns like to eat hard breads, such as Finn Crisps which are familiar to Americans. Children like hard bread, which is very good for their teeth. The old generation of hard-bread eaters, who also rarely had sugar, didn't have our problem with cavities.

I find gluten flour, available in well-stocked health food stores, the best base for yeast and other breads. It gives a texture that comes closest to the original Finnish breads. If you want, substitute a good hard wheat flour, especially meant for bread baking, if you can get it.

There are two other terms used frequently in these recipes: unbleached white flour, and unbleached white pastry flour. The unbleached white flour is a general name for the unbleached flour that one buys in health food stores. In some recipes, mainly in pie crust and cookie recipes, I have specified the kind of flour that produces the best results: the unbleached white pastry flour. It is made of soft wheat and gives a light, crisp texture; very little gluten is formed in the flour. Ordinary unbleached white flour may be substituted, with almost as good results.

Breads

Rye bread is the favorite bread of the Finns, especially sour rye. It is the most nourishing of all breads. The yeast breads are mixtures of several grains, which blend in a wonderful way.

If you are hesitant with yeast—many people feel it's capricious—start with the flat breads, which are the oldest form of bread, made so for centuries. These breads are mostly regional breads, from all over Finland.

PULLA, THE BASIC SWEET BREAD [PULLA]

You find *pulla* on every Finnish coffee table and in every bakery shop. The smell of freshly baked *pulla* equals the smell of home in people's minds. Everyone has a slightly different recipe, and it can be made either plain or fancy, seasoned with sugar and cinnamon or saffron, and sprinkled with sugar, almonds, or both.

1 cup milk, scalded	½ cup melted butter
2 tablespoons active dry yeast	2/3 cup raw sugar
2 eggs	1 teaspoon ground cardamom
1½ teaspoons sea salt	½ cup raisins (optional)
2 cups gluten flour	2–2-1/3 cups unbleached white flour

Glaze:
  1 egg   Raw sugar

Cool the scalded milk until it is warm. Dissolve the yeast in it. Beat the eggs lightly, add to the milk. Add salt and 1 cup of the gluten flour. Beat the dough well.

Add the melted butter and 1 cup gluten flour. Beat well. Add the sugar, cardamom, and raisins, if used. Knead in the pastry flour. Use 2 cups at first, and add more flour in very small portions, if necessary. The dough should feel soft and elastic to the hand, and never be too hard. Knead well until the dough makes smacking sounds when you pull out your knuckles, about 20 minutes.

On a baking board, divide the dough into two parts. You may use one part for making small, round rolls. Divide the rest of the dough into three equal parts, roll them into long strips, and make a braid. Put the rolls and the braid on lightly floured baking sheets. Cover with towels, and let rise in a warm place until well doubled in size. Since the bread is allowed to rise only once, it should be done well, about 1½ hours.

Meanwhile, preheat the oven to 400°F. Brush the breads with the beaten egg, and sprinkle with sugar. Bake rolls 10 to 15 minutes, or until golden. The braid will take 15 to 20 minutes. Take out from the oven, cover with a towel to let them soften, and cool.

Serve warm for breakfast with jam, or with coffee or for dessert with dessert soups. Freeze what you don't eat immediately, because it will dry up quickly, if not frozen. Warm the frozen *pulla*, wrapped in foil, in the oven.

Use of leftovers: Dry leftover braids for rusks (see page 161), or for Poor Knights (see page 141), or Bread Pudding (see page 143).

Yield: 10 rolls and 1 braid.

SOUR RYE BREAD [HAPANLEIPÄ]

This is another basic Finnish bread. It can be made of rye flour only, but it's rather troublesome to handle. The gluten flour gives firmness to the dough.

1 tablespoon active dry yeast
4 cups lukewarm water
7 cups rye flour

1¾ cups gluten flour
1 tablespoon sea salt

Start by making the sour starter 2 days in advance. Dissolve the yeast in warm water. Add 2 cups rye flour, and beat well to make a soupy mixture. Sprinkle the top of the bowl with rye flour. Keep in a warm place 1 full day. It will ferment and become sour. A good place to keep it is on the pilot of a gas stove, which is covered with an asbestos plate. Cover the dough with a towel.

The second day, add 2 more cups rye flour, stir well, and let stand 1 more day. The starter will appear very sour, but don't be disturbed.

Now to make the bread, add the gluten flour to the starter, and beat well to give the dough some shape. Rye flour is sticky and hard to work with. Add more rye flour, but do not exceed the amount given. Knead well, about ½ hour, until the dough ceases to be sticky and gets some elasticity.

With damp hands, make a ball of the dough. Put it into a bowl, sprinkle with flour, and let rise until doubled in size, 1 to 1½ hours.

Knead the dough again, for about 15 minutes. It should be easier to handle. Let rise again another hour, or until doubled.

Preheat the oven to 450°F. With damp hands, form 2 round loaves, or 3 flat round ones in which you cut the center away with a large cookie cutter to form a large doughnut-shaped loaf. Prick the loaves with a fork; make wedge marks on the round breads. Put on a floured baking sheet, cover, and let rise until almost doubled.

Bake the loaves 1 hour, the doughnut-shaped breads about 45 minutes. Take out and cover with a couple of heavy towels, to soften the crust. It will still be hard and crisp—the best part of the bread.

Yield: 2 to 3 loaves.

BUTTERMILK LOAF [PIIMÄLIMPPU]

The taste is slightly sweet; excellent for sandwiches. This bread keeps well even unfrozen.

½ cup blackstrap or ordinary
* molasses*
1½ cups buttermilk
2 tablespoons active dry yeast
½ cup warm water
1 tablespoon sea salt

1 teaspoon ground caraway
* seeds*
1 teaspoon ground orange peel
2 cups gluten flour
2½–2¾ cups rye flour

Glaze:
1 tablespoon molasses

1 tablespoon water

Put the molasses into a saucepan, bring to a boil, and remove from heat. Cool a little. Warm the buttermilk, but be careful not to overheat, or it will separate.

Dissolve the yeast in warm water. Add molasses and warm buttermilk. Throw in the salt, caraway seeds, and orange peel. Add gluten flour, and beat well. Knead in the rye flour. Knead well, until the dough doesn't stick to your hand or the bowl, 20 to 30 minutes. Add more rye flour, if necessary.

Form the dough into a ball, put into a bowl, cover, and let rise in a warm place until doubled in bulk, 1 to 1½ hours. Punch down, and knead on a baking board. Preheat the oven to 425°F. Divide the dough into two parts. Oil two 1-quart loaf pans, shape the dough into two oval loaves, and put them into the loaf pans. Prick with fork. Cover, and let rise in a warm place until almost doubled.

Bake the loaves 40 to 50 minutes. When they have been in the oven 20 minutes, brush the tops with a mixture of molasses and water. Take them out of the oven, cover, and let cool.
  Yield: 2 loaves.

SEASONED YEAST BREAD [MAUSTETTU HIIVALEIPÄ]

1 cup water, whey, or other liquid
1 cup buttermilk
2 tablespoons active dry yeast
1½ teaspoons sea salt
½ teaspoon ground fennel or
* aniseed*

½ teaspoon ground caraway seeds
1-2/3 cups gluten flour
1½ cups barley flour
1 cup rye flour

Combine the water or other liquid, and buttermilk. Heat until warm. Dissolve the yeast into the liquid. Add the salt, aniseed or fennel, and caraway seeds. Add the gluten flour, beating well until it thickens. Add the barley flour little by little, and knead in enough rye flour to make smooth dough. Knead well, about 20 minutes.

Shape the dough into a ball, put into a bowl, and let rise, covered, in a warm place until doubled in bulk, 1 to 1½ hours. Punch down, and knead on a board.

Preheat the oven to 425°F. Divide the dough into two parts, and make two small round loaves. Put on a floured baking sheet, cover, and let rise until almost doubled in size, about 1 hour. Bake 30 to 40 minutes. Take out and cool uncovered on racks for a crisp crust.
  Yield: 2 loaves.

YEAST BREAD [HIIVALEIPÄ]

A good bread with soups, and great for dipping into pots and gravies.

2 cups water or whey, or potato
  boiling water
2 tablespoons active dry yeast
1½ teaspoons sea salt
1-2/3 cups gluten flour

1½ cups graham or whole wheat
  flour
1½ cups rye or barley flour
2 tablespoons melted butter or oil

Warm the water or other liquid, and dissolve the yeast in it. Add salt. Stir in gluten flour and beat well. Add the graham or whole wheat flour. Knead in the rye or barley flour. Keep kneading 20 minutes, until the dough is elastic and doesn't stick to your fingers. Knead in the butter or oil.

Make the dough into a ball, put into a bowl, cover, and let rise in a warm place until doubled in bulk, about 1 hour.

Preheat the oven to 425°F. Punch the dough down, and divide into two parts. Make two round loaves, and prick them with a fork. Put on a floured baking sheet, cover, and let rise until almost doubled, about 1 hour.

Bake the loaves 30 to 40 minutes. For a crisp crust, cool, uncovered, on racks.

Yield: 2 loaves.

GRAHAM BREAD [GRAHAMLEIPÄ]

2 cups water, whey, or potato
  boiling water
2 tablespoons active dry yeast

1½ teaspoons sea salt
2 cups gluten flour
2 cups graham or whole wheat flour

Warm the liquid, and dissolve the yeast in it. Add salt and beat in gluten flour. Beat until thick. Knead in the graham or whole wheat flour, and keep kneading until the dough is elastic and makes smacking sounds, about 20 minutes.

Put the dough into a bowl, cover, and let rise in a warm place until doubled in bulk, about 1 hour. Punch down on a baking board, divide into two parts, and make two round or oblong loaves. Cover, and let rise until almost doubled, about 1 hour.

Preheat the oven to 425°F. Bake the loaves 25 to 30 minutes. For crisp crust, cool uncovered on racks.

Yield: 2 loaves.

OAT FLOUR BREAD [KAURALEIPÄ]

A delicate, country-flavored bread. Eat it fresh—it doesn't keep very well.

2 cups water, whey, or vegetable
  boiling water
2 tablespoons active dry yeast
1½ teaspoons sea salt

2¼ cups gluten flour
1 tablespoon honey
3 cups oat flour

Warm the liquid and dissolve the yeast in it. Add salt and gluten flour; beat well until it thickens. Add the honey and as much oat flour as necessary to make an elastic, soft, and silky dough. Knead about 20 minutes. Put into a bowl, cover, and let rise in a warm place until doubled in bulk, about 1 hour.

Preheat the oven to 425°F. Punch the dough down, and divide into two round loaves, and prick with a fork. Cover, and let rise until almost doubled. Bake 25 to 30 minutes. For crisp crust, cool uncovered on racks.
   Yield: 2 loaves.

BARLEY FLOUR BREAD [OHRALEIPÄ]

1 cup water
1 cup buttermilk
2 tablespoons active dry yeast
1½ teaspoons sea salt

2 cups gluten flour
¼ cup melted butter or good oil
2–2-1/3 cups barley flour

Mix the water and buttermilk. Warm, but do not overheat, or the buttermilk will separate. Dissolve the yeast in it. Add salt and beat in gluten flour. Beat until it thickens. Add butter or oil, and knead in the barley flour. Add 2 cups at first, and then more, little by little, up to 2-1/3 cups, or until it's easy to handle. Knead well, about 20 minutes.

Shape the dough into a ball, put into a bowl, cover, and let rise in a warm place until doubled in bulk, about 1 hour.

Preheat the oven to 425°F. Divide the dough into two round loaves, and cut 3 slits across each. Cover, and let rise on a baking sheet until almost doubled. Bake 30 to 40 minutes. Cool on a rack.
   Yield: 2 loaves.

HEALTH BREAD [TERVEYSLEIPÄ]

1 cup cracked wheat (sometimes
   called wheat pilaf)
1½ cups buttermilk, at room
   temperature
2½ tablespoons active dry yeast
1 cup warm water

1½ teaspoons sea salt
2 cups gluten flour
¼ cup oil or melted butter
1¼ cups rye flour
¾–1 cup unbleached white flour

Soak the cracked wheat in buttermilk a couple of hours, or until soft. Dissolve the yeast into warm water. Add the salt and 1 cup gluten flour to the yeast mixture. Beat well. Stir in the oil or melted butter. Add 1 cup gluten flour. Knead in the cracked wheat mixture and rye flour. Finally, little by little, knead in the unbleached white flour. Use just enough to make a soft, elastic dough. Knead about 20 minutes. Let rise, covered, in a warm place until doubled in bulk.

Preheat the oven to 425°F. Punch the dough down, and shape into two oblong loaves. Let rise until almost doubled, about 1 hour. Bake 20 to 30 minutes. For crisp crust, cool on racks.
   Yield: 2 loaves.

WHITE ATTIC BREAD [VINTTIKAKKO]

The small flat loaves are much like the Syrian bread known in America, but richer.

½ cup milk
½ cup light cream
1 tablespoon dry active yeast
1 teaspoon sea salt

1 teaspoon ground aniseed
½ cup gluten flour
1¾ cups unbleached white flour

Scald the milk and cream, and cool until warm. Dissolve the yeast in it, add salt and aniseed. Add the gluten flour, beat well. Knead in the white flour. The dough should be soft and elastic, a little harder than pizza dough. Knead well, and form into a ball. Let rise, covered, until doubled in bulk.

Preheat the oven to 375°F. Divide the dough into two flat round breads, about 9 inches across. Prick all over with a fork. Cut a cross on the breads. Bake 15 to 20 minutes. Cool covered.
    Yield: 2 loaves.

BARLEY FLAT BREAD [OHRARIESKA]

This is a thick, chewy bread with a subtly sour taste. It is good with soups, or as a snack, or as a coffee bread, spread with butter.

1 cup pearl or hulled barley
¼ cup barley flour
2½ cups buttermilk

1 egg, lightly beaten
1½ teaspoons sea salt
1 tablespoon oil or butter

Let the barley and barley flour soak in the buttermilk 7 to 8 hours, or overnight. Keep the bowl at room temperature.

Preheat the oven to 350°F. Grease a square glass cake pan. Add the lightly beaten egg and salt to the barley-buttermilk mixture, mix well. Pour into the pan. Bake 1 to 1½ hours. After ½ hour, brush the top with butter or oil. The top and sides should be brown and crisp. Serve warm or cold.
    Yield: 1 loaf.

OAT FLAT BREAD [KAURARIESKA]

You may make this either as a flat bread, or a version more like a pancake, to be eaten with jam, with coffee or as a dessert.

Bread:
1½ cups rolled oats   1 egg, lightly beaten
1½ cups buttermilk   Oil or butter
 ½ teaspoon sea salt

Pancake:
 1 cup rolled oats   ½ teaspoon raw sugar or honey
 2 cups buttermilk   2 eggs, lightly beaten
 ½ teaspoon sea salt   Oil or butter

Soak the oats in the buttermilk until the buttermilk has been absorbed.

Preheat the oven to 350°F. Butter a square glass cake pan. Add the salt, sugar or honey, if used, and lightly beaten egg(s) to the buttermilk mixture. Pour into the pan. Bake about 1 hour. After baking ½ hour, brush the top with oil or butter.

BACON FLAT BREAD [PEKONIRIESKA]

This is a quick bread that comes out the same every time. Eat with light soups.

4 thick strips bacon, cut into   2 cups barley flour
   small cubes   ½ teaspoon sea salt, or to taste
2 cups milk

Preheat the oven to 500°F. Brown the bacon cubes in a frying pan, until crisp and brown. With a slotted spoon, remove the bacon, and drain on paper towels. Save the bacon fat.

Grease a 9-inch round cake pan with some of the bacon fat. A heavy glass pan is best. Mix the milk and barley flour into a smooth loose dough, add salt and the rest of the bacon fat and bacon cubes. Pour the dough into the cake pan, flatten out with a spoon. Bake 15 to 20 minutes. There should be little dark brown spots on the surface of the bread when it's ready. Turn out from the pan, cut into wedges, and serve warm or cold.

POTATO FLAT BREAD [PERUNARIESKA]

An old specialty with real country flavor. Treat your guests with it—it's a true delicacy.

½ lb potatoes   1/3 cup gluten flour
 2 cups water   1 cup barley flour
 1 teaspoon sea salt

Boil the potatoes in their jackets in 2 cups water, until soft. Reserve the cooking liquid. Peel the potatoes and mash while still hot. Add 1 cup cooking liquid. Mix well, and let cool. Put into the refrigerator and chill.

Preheat the oven to 550°F. Add salt to the potato mixture. Add gluten flour, and beat well. Knead in the barley flour. Knead 10 to 15 minutes. Shape the dough into a ball. Dip your hands in cold water if the dough is hard to handle.

Grease a large baking sheet with oil or butter. Pat the dough ball down until it becomes a large, thin round or oval layer that fills the baking sheet almost completely. It should be about ¼ inch thick. Prick all over with a fork.

Bake 15 to 20 minutes. The bread should have dark brown spots all over, and the edges should be dark brown and crisp, almost burned.

Take the bread out, cover with a towel for 10 to 20 minutes to soften a little. Cut into squares and serve while still oven-warm. Spread with butter.

HARD BREAD I [NÄKKILEIPÄ I]

This bread is truly hard and rye-flavored. It is a Western Finland bread.

2 cups water or whey	1½ teaspoons sea salt
1 tablespoon dry active yeast	4½ cups rye flour

Start the dough the night before. Dissolve the yeast in warm water or whey. Add salt and 2 cups of the flour. Beat well. Let the dough stand in a warm place overnight.

Next day, beat the dough well. Add the rest of the flour, about 2½ cups. Knead well and shape into a ball. Let rise, covered, in a warm place for about 1 hour.

Preheat the oven to 475°F. Punch the dough down and divide it into 4 equal parts. On a well-floured board, roll each part out thin. Each one should be about the size of a baking sheet.

Put on cookie sheets. With a pizza cutter, mark the dough into squares so that it will be easy to break along the lines. Prick the surface of the bread with a fork. Bake about 15 minutes.

Let the breads cool on racks to dry. If they tend to bend, put weights on the breads to keep them from curling. Keep the breads in a dry, cool place to prevent them from getting soggy.

HARD BREAD II [NÄKKILEIPÄ II]

1 cup milk	1 teaspoon sea salt
2 tablespoons active dry yeast	1 cup gluten flour
1 cup rye flour	¼ cup melted butter or oil

Start the night before. Scald the milk, and let cool to warm. Dissolve the yeast in it, and add the rye flour. Beat well. Let stand in a warm place, covered, overnight.

Next day, add the salt and gluten flour. Knead in melted butter or oil. Knead well until the dough is smooth and elastic. Shape into a ball, put into a warm place, and let rise, covered, until doubled in bulk.

Preheat the oven to 450°F. Punch the dough down, and divide into 4 parts. Roll each part out with a light hand. Roll into a square as thin as you can without breaking the dough. Prick the surface of the bread sheets with a fork. With a pizza cutter, make square marks. Put on cookie sheets, and let rise ½ hour. Bake 10 to 15 minutes. Do not let burn.

Cool on racks. Keep the hard, crisp breads in a cool, dry place.

BUCKWHEAT FLAT BREAD [TATTARLEIPÄ]

An old Karelian recipe. There were special bakers who were known for their buckwheat bread, and they came to private homes to bake for big occasions.

½ lb potatoes	2 cups buckwheat flour
3 cups water	½ cup buttermilk
½ teaspoon sea salt	1 cup gluten flour
1 tablespoon yeast	1½ teaspoons sea salt
1/3 cup warm water	Egg or butter (optional)

Start making the dough 1 day before serving. Boil the potatoes, in their jackets, in salted water until soft. Reserve the cooking liquid. Peel the potatoes and mash while still warm. Add 2 cups cooking liquid, mix well.

Pour the potato mixture through a sieve into a bowl. Let cool. Mix the yeast into warm water, and add to the potatoes. Add 1 cup buckwheat flour. Let stand in a warm place 6 to 7 hours or overnight. The dough will ferment.

Add the buttermilk to the dough, and 1 cup buckwheat flour. Stir in gluten flour. Season with salt. The dough should be the consistency of a thick porridge.

Preheat the oven to 450°F. Grease well a heavy baking pan that has high edges. Pour the dough in, and spread a little to make it about 1 inch thick. Bake 20 to 30 minutes. When half done, brush with egg or butter, if you want. Cut into squares and serve warm.

Rolls and Rusks

Rolls and rusks are made from the same basic dough, which is made softer than bread doughs with more yeast. Use the rolls as dinner rolls, hamburger buns, sandwiches, or snacks. Eat the crunchy rusks as substitutes for crackers and cookies, spread them with jam or cheese, serve as snacks, with coffee or tea.

To dry rusks, let the ready baked rolls cool a little, until comfortable to handle. Split them into halves with a fork. Heat the oven to 450°F. Put the split rolls on cookie sheets, split side up. Bake about 10 minutes, or until lightly browned. Lower the heat to 200–225°F, and dry the rusks 1 to 1½ hours, or until light, dry, and crisp. Keep rusks in an air-tight container, in a cool, dry place.

GRAHAM ROLLS OR RUSKS
[GRAHAMSÄMPYLÄT TAI –KORPUT]

1 cup milk	2 oz (½ stick) butter, softened
1½ tablespoons active dry yeast	¼ cup brown sugar
1 teaspoon sea salt	1¼ cups graham or whole wheat flour
1¼ cups gluten flour	

Scald the milk and let cool to lukewarm. Dissolve the yeast in it. Add salt, and gluten flour. Beat well until it thickens. Beat the softened butter and brown sugar together until foamy. Add to the dough. Knead in the graham or whole wheat flour. Knead well, about 20 minutes.

Shape the dough into a ball, and let rise, covered, in a warm place until well doubled in bulk, about 1 hour.

Preheat the oven to 425°F. Punch the dough down, and knead on a baking board. Shape into a long tube, and divide into 10 to 15 equal pieces. Roll small, round balls, and put them on a floured baking sheet. Cover, and let rise until almost doubled in size. Bake 10 to 15 minutes.

If you want rolls, cover and cool, and freeze, or you can make rusks (see page 158).
  Yield: 10 to 15 rolls.

OAT ROLLS OR RUSKS [KAURASÄMPYLÄT TAI –KORPUT]

1½ tablespoons active dry yeast	1¾ cups gluten flour
1 cup milk, scalded	1/3 cup melted butter or oil
1 teaspoon sea salt	2 cups rolled oats
2 tablespoons honey, warmed	

Dissolve the yeast in the scalded, warm milk. Add the salt and warm honey. Beat in about half of the gluten flour: beat well until it thickens. Add the butter or oil, and the rest of gluten flour. Knead in the rolled oats. Knead about 20 minutes.

Shape the dough into a ball, and let rise, covered, in a warm place until doubled in bulk, about 1 hour.

Punch the dough down, and knead into a long tube. Divide into 15 equal pieces. Roll them into small, round balls, put on a baking sheet, and let rise, covered, until doubled in size. Meanwhile, preheat the oven to 425°F. Bake about 15 minutes.

Take out, cover, and let cool a little. If you want rolls, freeze them. For making rusks, see page 158.
  Yield: about 15 rolls.

HEALTH ROLLS OR RUSKS
[TERVEYSSÄMPYLÄT TAI –KORPUT]

1-2/3 cups milk, scalded
  2 tablespoons active dry yeast
1½ teaspoons sea salt
2¼ cups gluten flour
  2 tablespoons raw sugar

½ teaspoon ground aniseed
¾ cup barley flour
½ cup rye flour
2 oz (½ stick) butter, softened

Cool the scalded milk until it is warm, and dissolve the yeast in it. Add salt and beat in half of the gluten flour. Beat well. Add the sugar, aniseed, the rest of the gluten flour, and then, kneading, add the barley and rye flour. Knead well, about 20 minutes. Knead in the softened butter.

Shape the dough into a ball, and let rise, covered, in a warm place until doubled in bulk, about 1 hour.

Preheat the oven to 425°F. Punch the dough down, and make into a long tube. Divide it into about 15 parts. Roll into small, round balls; put them on a floured baking sheet. Cover with a towel, and let rise until doubled in size. Bake 15 minutes. Cover and cool the rolls, and freeze. For making rusks, see page 158.

Yield: 15 rolls.

SEASONED ROLLS OR RUSKS
[MAUSTESÄMPYLÄT TAI –KORPUT]

1-2/3 cups milk, scalded
  2 tablespoons active dry yeast
¼ cup blackstrap or ordinary
  molasses
1 teaspoon ground orange peel
½ teaspoon ground aniseed
½ teaspoon ground fennel

1 teaspoon sea salt
1-2/3 cups gluten flour
1 cup unbleached white flour
¾–1 cup rye flour
½ cup (1 stick) melted butter
  or oil

Cool the scalded milk to warm, and dissolve the yeast in it. In a saucepan, combine the molasses, orange peel, aniseed, and fennel. Bring to a quick boil, and cool. Add the salt and cooled molasses to the milk and yeast. Beat in the gluten flour; beat well to make it thicken. Add the unbleached white flour, and knead in rye flour. Knead well, about 20 minutes.

Shape the dough into a ball, and let rise, covered, in a warm place until doubled in bulk, 1 to 1½ hours.

Punch the dough down on a board. Form into a long tube, and divide into 15 to 20 parts. Roll into small round balls. Put on a floured baking sheet, cover, and let rise until doubled in size.

Preheat the oven to 425°F. Bake the rolls about 15 minutes. Cover and let cool. Freeze the rolls. For making rusks, see page 158.

Yield: 15 to 20 rolls.

CINNAMON RUSKS [KANELIKORPUT]

15–20 slices leftover pulla (see page 150) or white bread
3 tablespoons raw sugar

1 teaspoon cinnamon
1–2 egg whites, beaten

Mix together the sugar and cinnamon. Preheat the oven to 225°F. Brush the bread slices with egg white, and dip them into the cinnamon-sugar mixture, coating on both sides.

Put the coated bread on cookie sheets. Let dry in the oven, about 1¼ hours. Take out and let cool on sheets. When cooled, store in a dry, cool place. Serve the crunchy rusks with coffee.

Dinner Pies and Pastries

Pie making is an art that the Karelians are known for. Many of these whole-meal pie recipes have equals in Russian cooking; there is only a slight difference in the Finnish way of making them. The large pies, with a fish, meat, or vegetable filling are festive enough for entrees at special dinners, and are certainly mouth-watering.

The classic and troublesome puff pastry can, of course, be used as a crust for these recipes, but I prefer to make the crusts as given here. They are quicker and easier to make, and are better from the viewpoint of nutrition. They are also interchangeable; but the crusts and fillings as combined in the following recipes do go very well together.

Roosters—a specialty of the Middle Finland province, Savo—are hearty food. They are actually an early form of canned food, and as that are very practical from the ecological point of view. The can—the thick rye crust—is eaten along with the filling. The roosters were often taken as provisions for long journeys, especially when one went to work in the woods or on faraway fields. Today roosters are eaten with the same enthusiasm as in the early days, but the main reason now is the taste.

OIL DOUGH FOR PASTRIES [ÖLJYTAIKINA]

For those who do not touch butter, here is an oil-based dough which may be substituted for the crusts of the pies. It is not anything close to the original crusts in taste; it is more difficult to handle and very crumbly.

4 cups unbleached white flour	½ teaspoon raw sugar
1½ teaspoons baking powder	¾ cup oil
1 teaspoon sea salt	¼ cup cold water

Mix together the flour, baking powder, salt, and sugar. Pour in the oil, stirring quickly to make it into a dough. Pour in the water, and form into a ball. Do not handle too much. Chill a couple of hours.

Roll out and use as you would any pie crust.

SALMON PIE [LOHIPIIRAKKA]

Close to the Russian classic, *Kulebjaka*, the salmon pie is a favorite dinner-party dish.

Crust:
  ½ lb (2 sticks) butter   ½ teaspoon sea salt
  2 cups unbleached white pastry   2–3 tablespoons cognac
    flour

Filling:
  3 hard-boiled eggs   1/3 cup chopped dill leaves
  2 cups cooked long-grain rice   ½ lb sliced lox

Glaze:
  1 egg, lightly beaten

Broth:
2/3 cup fish broth   2 oz (½ stick) butter, melted
2/3 cup beef broth   Chopped dill leaves

To make the crust, with a pastry cutter, cut the hard butter into the pastry flour, until the butter has become the size of dried peas. Add salt, and quickly pour in the cognac, shaping the dough into a ball that holds together, without handling the dough too much. Chill until hard.

Preheat the oven to 425°F. Divide the dough into two parts. While rolling the bottom crust, keep the other part in the refrigerator. Roll the dough on a floured board into a rectangle about 1/3 inch thick. Move it onto an oiled baking sheet. The pie will be about the size and shape of a 2-quart loaf pan.

Slice the hard-boiled eggs. To fill the pie, spread the rice on the bottom crust, leaving a little more than an inch empty at the sides. Try to keep the filling as close to a rectangle as possible. Top the rice with some dill. Then make a layer of the salmon slices, and top with dill. On the top, stack the egg slices.

Roll out the top crust. Cover the filling with it. Seal the edges well, turn them up, and seal again. If there is leftover dough, cut into strips and decorate the pie. Brush with egg. Prick the crust with fork. Bake 30 to 35 minutes.

Combine the broth ingredients in the order given, and heat.

Serve for dinner. Slice, and spoon the broth over the slices. Dry champagne is good with this!
Servings: 4 to 6.

MEAT PIE [LIHAPIIRAKKA]

Crust:

2 cups unbleached white pastry
  flour
½ teaspoon sea salt

1½ cups cold boiled potatoes, mashed
¼ lb (1 stick) butter
2–4 tablespoons ice water

Filling:

1 onion, chopped
1 tablespoon butter
1 lb ground beef
1/3 lb ground pork
1 cup beef broth

½ cup light cream
1½ teaspoons sea salt, or to taste
¼ teaspoon white pepper
1 cup boiled rice (preferably brown)

Glaze:

1 egg

To make the crust, mix the flour, salt, and cold mashed potatoes. Cut in the cold butter. Add the ice water, and shape the dough into a firm ball. Chill.

For the filling, brown the onion in butter, and add the ground beef and pork. Brown all. Add the beef broth, light cream, and salt and pepper, stir. Let simmer on low heat 15 minutes. There should be some liquid left in the pan. Add the rice to the mixture, and cool.

Roll out the crust. Divide the dough into two equal parts. Roll the bottom crust into a rectangle to fit into an 8 x 14 oven pan. Move the crust to a lightly oiled oven pan. Pour the filling on it, flatten it out, and leave about 1½ inches empty at the sides.

Roll out the top crust, and cover the filling. Seal the edges well, turn them up, and seal again. Decorate the pie with leftover strips of dough. Preheat the oven to 425°F. Prick the crust all over with a fork, and brush with some egg. Bake about 30 minutes.

Serve hot for dinner. Or cut smaller pieces and serve as appetizers.
Servings: 6 to 8 as a main course.

SAUERKRAUT PIE [HAPANKAALIPIIRAKKA]

Sauerkraut Filling:
- 4 cups sauerkraut, drained
- 1 tablespoon butter
- 1 tablespoon molasses
- ¼ cup beef broth or water

Crust:
- ½ lb (2 sticks) butter
- 1½ cups unbleached white pastry flour
- 1 cup curd (see page 188)
- 1 teaspoon sea salt
- 2 tablespoons ice water or cognac

Meatball Filling:
- 1 small onion, chopped
- Butter
- 1/3 cup bread crumbs
- ½ cup light cream
- 1 lb lean ground meat
- ½ teaspoon sea salt
- ¼ teaspoon white pepper
- ⅛ teaspoon allspice, or to taste
- 1 egg

Glaze:
- 1 egg

To make the sauerkraut filling, put the kraut into a saucepan with the butter, molasses, and broth or water. Cover, and hatch about ½ hour, on low heat. Cool. To make the crust, cut the hard butter into the pastry flour. Add curd, salt, and water or cognac. Mix well, and quickly shape into a firm ball. Chill.

To make the meatballs, brown the onion in a little butter and let cool a little. Soak the bread crumbs in light cream. Combine the meat, bread crumbs and light cream, onion, salt, pepper, allspice, and egg. Mix well with your hands, until the dough starts to stick to your hands and to the bowl. With wet hands, make about 20 meatballs. Put aside.

Now to make the pie, divide the crust into two parts, and on a well-floured board, roll out the bottom crust in a rectangle. It should be a little smaller than a baking pan. Lift the crust onto a lightly oiled oven pan. Spoon about half of the sauerkraut into the middle of the crust, leaving 1½ inches empty at the sides. On top of the sauerkraut, put a layer of 12 meatballs. Then the rest of the sauerkraut, and the rest of the meatballs.

Preheat the oven to 425°F. Roll out the top crust, and put on top of the filling. Seal the edges well, turn them up, and seal again. Let the pie harden in the refrigerator, for about 30 minutes.

Prick the crust with a fork, and brush with egg. Bake 30 to 35 minutes.

Cut into slices and serve as a main course.
Servings: 6 to 8.

CABBAGE PIE [KAALIPIIRAKKA]

The secret of this pie is in the treatment of the cabbage: fry it slowly, gently, but in a determined way. The result is a sweet and powerful taste that is loved by many.

Filling:

2 oz (½ stick) butter	3 tablespoons corn syrup or molasses
4 lbs cabbage (centers removed), chopped coarsely (see below)	2 tablespoons white vinegar
	1 teaspoon sea salt

Crust:

½ lb (2 sticks) hard butter	1 tablespoon white vinegar
3 cups unbleached white pastry flour	½ cup ice water

Glaze:
   1 egg

Brown the cabbage slowly; this is what brings out the delicious flavor. For this amount of cabbage, use two large, heavy iron frying pans. Divide the butter evenly between the two pans. The cabbage is cut into square pieces of about 1 inch—not grated or shredded. Brown the butter in the pan, and add the cabbage. In the beginning, keep the heat moderately low, and let the cabbage lose some liquid. Stir once in a while.

When the cabbage has shrunk a little, increase the heat. Now the cabbage should be browned evenly; not just golden, but nicely brown. It should become soft, but not limp and watery. The browning will take a good ½ hour. When the cabbage is brown, add the corn syrup or molasses and vinegar. Stir well. Remove from the pan, and cool.

To make the crust, cut the butter into the flour, until the grains are the size of small peas. Add vinegar and cold water, mixing quickly. Make a ball of dough. Chill.

Preheat the oven to 425°F. Divide the dough into two parts. On a floured board, roll out the bottom crust to the size of a baking sheet. The crust should be thin. Put the crust on a lightly greased baking sheet. Spoon the cabbage on the crust, leaving about 1½ inches empty at the sides. The finished pie will be about 1 inch thick. Roll out the top crust, place on top of the filling, and seal the edges well, turn up, and seal again.

Brush with egg, and prick with a fork. Bake about ½ hour.

Serve as a lunch dish, snack, sandwich, or an appetizer. It is as good warm as cold. Spread lightly with butter, if you want to indulge. In Finland cabbage pie with a glass of milk or beer is a favorite after-sauna food.

Servings: 8 to 10, or more as an appetizer.

FISH ROOSTER [KALAKUKKO]

Probably the best known, and best loved, of the roosters. A native of the Eastern Finland town Kuopio, the rooster is now known in the whole country. Fresh roosters arrive daily by the Kuopio train to the capital, Helsinki, where they are quickly sold out.

Crust:
4 cups rye flour
2 cups water
1/2–1 cup unbleached white flour
1 tablespoon salt
2 tablespoons melted butter

Filling:
1 1/2 lbs cleaned small fish (perch is often used)
1 teaspoon sea salt
1/2 lb thickly sliced bacon

Glaze:
Butter
Water

Mix the flour and water into a hard, firm, but pliable dough. Use more or less flour; the dough should be firm enough to be shaped, like clay. Add salt and melted butter. Knead the dough on a floured board, make it into a ball, and roll and pat it out into a 1 1/2-inch thick oval sheet.

Sprinkle the center with flour. Leave about 7 inches empty at the edges. Place half of the fish on the flour, sprinkle with salt, top with bacon; repeat.

Preheat the oven to 450°F. Fold the dough over the filling to make an oval, foot-ball-shaped package. Seal the edges using water, so that the juices cannot escape. Brush with a mixture of butter and water. (If the edges aren't sealed properly and the juices do escape, the rooster is said "to sing.")

Bake the rooster 1 1/2 hours. Turn the oven to 300°F. Wrap the rooster in alumi-num foil, and bake 2 1/2 to 3 more hours. Turn off the oven. Leave the rooster in the foil, wrap the package with many layers of newspaper. Put the package back into the oven, and let it hatch a few hours, preferably overnight. This hatching will soften the crust, and bones of the fish (which then become edible).

If served for dinner, the rooster is placed on a plate. A lid is cut off. Scoop the insides onto your plate, and cut a wedge of the crust to be eaten as bread. As a snack, or if you want to save part of the rooster, cut into slices like bread. This is a robust meal; accompany it with a cucumber salad (see page 114), nothing more.
Servings: 6 to 8 as a main course.

MEAT ROOSTER [LIHAKUKKO]

I like to wrap this rooster in sour dough, but the crust for fish rooster can be used as well.

Crust:
1 tablespoon active dry yeast   4 1/2–5 cups rye flour
2 cups warm water   1 1/2 teaspoons sea salt

Filling:

    1 lb beef, sliced (meat used for   1 teaspoon sea salt, or to taste
        stews is fine)   1/4 teaspoon white pepper
1/2–3/4 lb pork, sliced

Dissolve the yeast in warm water. Add 2 cups rye flour, beat well. Cover, and put the bowl in a warm place; let stand overnight to ferment.

Next day, add the salt and the rest of the rye flour, to make a firm but pliable dough. Knead on a floured board. With wet hands, form a ball, and flatten it out to an oval that's about 1 inch thick. Sprinkle the center with some rye flour, leaving about 6 inches empty at the sides.

In the middle, arrange a layer of beef, sprinkle with salt and pepper, top with pork, sprinkle with salt and pepper, and repeat. Preheat the oven to 450°F.

Fold the edges over the filling, to make an oval, football-shaped pie. Seal the seams well with water (see page 166). Put the rooster on a greased baking pan, and bake 1½ hours.

Lower the heat to 300°F. Wrap the rooster in foil, and bake 1½ more hours. Turn the oven off. Wrap the foil package in a thick layer of newspapers, and put back into the oven. Let hatch several hours, preferably overnight.

    Serve like fish rooster.
    Servings: 6 to 8.

RUTABAGA ROOSTER [LANTTUKUKKO]

The rooster brings out the sweetness of rutabaga. It's good eaten like a pie or sandwich.

Crust:

1½ cups water   3½ cups rye flour
    1 teaspoon sea salt   1/2 cup unbleached white flour

Filling:

    1 lb rutabaga, peeled and sliced   6 strips thickly sliced bacon
        into 1/2-inch pieces   1 tablespoon butter

Glaze:

    Water   Butter

Boil the rutabaga slices in a small amount of lightly salted water until almost done, or steam them. Discard the water, cool the rutabaga.

Make a firm, but pliable dough of the water, salt, and flour. Knead the dough on a floured board, and with wet hands, shape it into a ball. Flatten out to an oval, about 1 inch thick.

Preheat the oven to 450°F. Sprinkle the center of the crust with some flour. On it, layer the rutabaga slices. Leave about 5 inches empty at the sides. Cover with bacon and thin slices of butter; repeat. Make the top layers narrower than the first ones.

Fold the crust over the filling, and seal the edges using water so that the seam becomes invisible. Brush with a mixture of water and butter. Bake 1½ hours.

Turn the heat to 300°F. Wrap the rooster in foil. Bake 1½ more hours. Turn off the oven, wrap the foil package in thick layers of newspaper, and put back into the oven. Let hatch several hours, or overnight.

Serve like fish rooster (see page 166).
Servings: 6 to 8.

EGG OR MEAT PASTRIES [MUNA– TAI LIHAPASTEIJAT]

Eat these little pastries with hot broths or as snacks. These two fillings are the best known in Finland.

Crust:
¼ lb (1 stick) hard butter
1 cup unbleached white pastry flour
½ cup curd, pressed through a
sieve (see page 188)

½ teaspoon sea salt
1 tablespoon ice water or cognac

Egg Filling:
2/3 cup cooked rice

1 hard-boiled egg, chopped

Meat Filling:
2/3 cup cooked chopped meat
1/3 cup cooked rice

½ teaspoon sea salt, or to taste

Glaze:
1 egg or egg white

Make the crust by cutting the hard butter into the flour until it is in small grains. Add salt and curd, mix. Add water or cognac, and shape the mixture quickly into a firm ball. Chill.

Combine the ingredients of the filling you choose to use. Preheat the oven to 450°F. On a floured board, roll the crust out into a sheet about ¼ inch thick. With a cookie form or drinking glass of about 4 inches in diameter, cut out circles. On one half of each circle put about 1 teaspoon filling. Fold the other side over to form a half-moon shape. Press the edges together, seal with a fork or with fingers.

Brush the tops with egg or egg white. Put the pastries on a lightly greased baking sheet. Bake until nicely browned, about 10 minutes.

Serve warm with soup, broth, or tea. The egg pastries are great with salmon soup (see page 45), the meat pastries are usually eaten with a cup of bouillon. Do not freeze the pastries, reheating will make them soggy. That's why the recipe is a small one.
Yield: 10 to 12 pastries.

KARELIAN PASTRIES [KARJALANPIIRAKAT]

Another present-day favorite that has a long tradition behind it. The skill of the cooks in the old days was measured by the grace with which they rolled out the paper-thin crusts and folded the pretty pastries. But even the imperfectly-shaped ones taste delicious.

Crust:
1 cup water
2–2½ cups rye flour
1 teaspoon sea salt

Rice filling:
Rice porridge (see page 10)

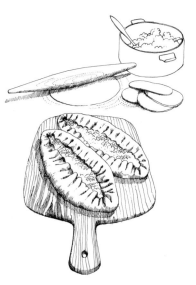

Potato filling:
2 lbs potatoes, boiled and mashed
1½ cups milk
½ teaspoon sea salt
1 tablespoon butter

To Dip:
Water
Butter

For the crust, mix the water, salt, and flour into a hard, but pliable dough. Knead well, and chill to make it more workable. Make either one of the fillings, and let cool.

To make the potato filling, combine the ingredients in the order given.

Roll the crust into a sheet about ¼ inch thick. With a round cookie form or drinking glass about 3 inches in diameter, cut out circles. Dust a little with flour, and stack to prevent drying.

When you have used all the dough, start rolling the round cakes out into paper-thin crusts. Flour the board heavily. They should be 5 to 7 inches in diameter. Stack the crusts, and cover with a towel to prevent drying.

Preheat the oven to 450°F. Fill the crusts. Put 1 heaping tablespoon of the filling in the middle of the crust. Leave about 1 inch empty at the sides. Then fold the sides over the filling, leaving some filling to show in the middle. This is how you fold: first make the boat-shaped pastries with two sharp ends. Then fold the sides, toward the center, pinching and making neat pleats. Pat down the sharp pleats to prevent them from burning.

Place the pastries on lightly greased cookie sheets. Bake 20 to 30 minutes. Pastries are done when the filling is browned. The crust will be very hard at this point.

While baking, heat some water and throw in 1 or 2 tablespoons of butter. Keep warm. When the pastries are ready, dip them into the water and butter, using tongs. Place them on a large dish, side by side, and cover immediately with a heavy towel. Dipping will give them a shiny surface, and covering will soften them.

Serve warm, with butter or egg-butter which is made by blending equal parts of butter and chopped hard-boiled egg. Good as snacks, eaten as sandwiches, with soups, or eaten as a first course, for lunch, and with tea or coffee.

Yield: 20 to 25 pastries.

Sweet Pies and Tarts

These fruit and berry pies differ from the American ones in that they are large, flat, and without a top crust. The crust is made either of *pulla* dough or a butter crust. The *pulla*-crust pies are usually made at the same time as *pulla* is baked, because to make a small amount of the dough would not be very practical.

The fillings are always simple, but the trick is to make them stay juicy, and at the same time sweet and tart. Blueberry pie is everyone's summer love, and after the first blueberries have come out, there are many blue-mouthed pie eaters around.

APPLE PIE [OMENAPIIRAKKA]

Crust:
2¼ cups unbleached white pastry
   flour
½ teaspoon baking powder

½ teaspoon sea salt
1 cup cream, whipped
¼ lb (1 stick) butter, softened

Filling:
  3 cups tart, juicy apple sauce

Glaze:
  1 egg

Combine the flour, baking powder, and salt. Stir them into the whipped cream. Knead in the softened butter, and shape the dough into a ball. Chill several hours.

Preheat the oven to 425°F. On a floured board, roll out the stiff crust into a square sheet, about the size of a baking sheet. Cut along the edges to make a regular square. Spread the filling over crust, leaving about 1½ inches empty at the sides.

Cut the leftover crust into long strips, and arrange them across the filling, to make squares. Turn the edges over the filling, seal corners. Brush edges and strips with egg.

Bake 20 to 25 minutes.

MOTHER'S APPLE PIE [ÄIDIN OMENAPIIRAKKA]

Crust:
1½ cups pulla dough without the
   raisins (see page 150)

Filling:
5–6 tart, juicy apples, peeled, cored,
   and sliced
2–3 tablespoons raw sugar
½ teaspoon cinnamon

2 eggs
2/3 cup milk
¼ teaspoon vanilla extract

Glaze:
  1 egg

Form the *pulla* dough into a ball. Flatten it out like a pizza, leaving the sides a little higher. Preheat the oven to 350°F. Let the crust rise about ½ hour. Flatten the center.

Fill the crust with apple slices, leaving the edges empty. There should be at least 2 layers of apple slices. Sprinkle them with sugar and dust with cinnamon. Beat the eggs lightly, add milk and vanilla. Pour this mixture over the apple slices.

Brush the crust with egg. Bake the pie 45 minutes to 1 hour, or until the eggs have set, but are not dried out. Cover the pie with a towel, and cool. Eat warm or cold.

BLUEBERRY PIE [MUSTIKKAPIIRAKKA]

Crust:
1½–2 cups pulla *dough without the*
  raisins (see page 150)

Filling:
  2 *pints blueberries*   2–3 *tablespoons raw sugar*
  1 *tablespoon potato starch*
  (see Note)

Glaze:
  1 *egg*

Preheat the oven to 400°F. Shape the *pulla* dough into a ball, and flatten it out like pizza. Make the pie into a square or an oval, almost the size of a cookie sheet. Put it on a lightly greased cookie sheet. Let rise about ½ hour. Flatten the center.

Mix together the blueberries and potato starch, so that the blueberries are coated. Spoon the blueberries over the crust, leaving about 2 inches empty at the edges. Sprinkle the blueberries with sugar. Use the leftover strips of dough to decorate the pie: run them across the filling. Brush the crust with egg. Bake the pie 20 to 30 minutes.

  Note: In a rainy year, the blueberries are more watery, and you may need a little more starch to hold the filling.

RHUBARB PIE [RAPERPERIPIIRAKKA]

Crust:
>   Crust for Apple Pie (see page
>   170), or 1½ cups pulla dough,
>   without raisins (see page 150)

Filling:
4–5 cups rhubarb, diced   4 tablespoons raw sugar

Glaze:
>   1 egg

Preheat the oven to 400°F. Prepare the crust as directed. Shape the dough into a ball, and flatten out like a pizza; or roll the butter dough into a square. Put the crust on a lightly greased cookie sheet. Let *pulla* dough rise about ½ hour; flatten the center.

Spread the rhubarb on the crust, and sprinkle with sugar. There should be a thick layer of rhubarb, so that it'll turn out juicy. Turn the edges of the crust up. Decorate the pie with leftover strips of dough. Bake about 20 minutes. Cool, and chill. Before eating, sprinkle with more sugar if necessary. The pie should be rather tart.

CRANBERRY OR LINGONBERRY PIES
[KARPALO- TAI PUOLUKKAPIIRAKAT]

Crust:
>   1 cup milk   1 cup gluten flour
>   1 tablespoon active dry yeast   ½ cup unbleached white flour
>   1 teaspoon sea salt   2/3 cup rye flour

Filling:
2–2½ cups mashed cranberries or   Raw sugar to taste, if mashed
>   cranberry or lingonberry   berries are used
>   preserves

Glaze:
>   ¼ cup water   1 teaspoon raw sugar

Scald the milk, let cool to warm, and dissolve the yeast in it. Add salt and gluten flour, and beat until thick. Knead in the unbleached white pastry flour and rye flour, to make a smooth, elastic dough. Knead well. Let rise in a warm place until doubled in bulk, about 1 hour.

Preheat the oven to 425°F. Punch the dough down, and divide it into 8 equal parts. Shape each part into a ball, and let rise until doubled. Punch down the balls in the middle, making room for the filling.

Fill the pies with the berry filling. Bake about 15 minutes. While baking, brush the crusts a couple of times with the water and sugar mixture.

Take the pies out, brush once more, and cover with towels to soften. Eat cold.
   Servings: 8 individual pies.

CURD PIE [RAHKAPIIRAKKA]

A great pie that reminds one of the *pasha*. Good with coffee, or as a dessert.

Filling:
   2 cups curd, from 2 quarts
      buttermilk (see page 188)
   1 cup sour cream
   3 tablespoons raw sugar

   Grated peel and juice of 1 lemon
   ¼ *cup raisins*
   ¼ *teaspoon vanilla extract*
   2 *eggs*

Crust:
   2 cups pulla *dough, without the*
   raisins (see page 150)

Glaze:
   1 egg

To make the filling, combine ingredients and beat to make an even mixture.

Shape the *pulla* dough into a ball, and flatten out into an oval about the size of a cookie sheet. Put it on a lightly greased sheet. Let rise. Punch down the center. Preheat the oven to 350°F. Spoon the filling over the crust, and turn the edges up. Brush the crust with egg. Bake about ½ hour. Cool. Serve cold.

STRAWBERRY CURD TART [MANSIKKA-RAHKATORTTU]

Crust:
   ¼ *lb (1 stick) butter, softened*
   ¼ *cup raw sugar*

   1/3 *cup unbleached white flour*
   1½ *cups rolled oats*

Filling:
   1 cup curd, from 1 quart buttermilk
      (see page 188)
   2 tablespoons cream

   ¼ *cup orange juice*
   1 *tablespoon raw sugar*
   1 *pint sweet, ripe strawberries*

Preheat the oven to 400°F. Whip the softened butter and sugar until light and foamy. Add the flour and rolled oats. Mix well. Grease a 9-inch cake pan and pat the crust down into it. Bake 15 to 20 minutes. Cool.

Combine all the ingredients for the filling, except the strawberries. Beat well. Clean and halve the strawberries. Spoon the filling over the cool crust. Cover with strawberry halves. Cut into wedges and serve.

OLD KARELIAN EGG PIE [MUNAPIIRAKKA]

This pie used to be a special Sunday treat: it was only for occasions that one would have all the eggs, cream, and sugar to spare.

Crust:
  1 cup pulla *dough, without the*
  raisins (see page 150)

Glaze:
  1 *egg*

Filling:
  3 *eggs*   ½ *cup cream*
  ½ *cup raw sugar*

Preheat the oven to 350°F. Flatten the dough into a circle about 11 inches in diameter. Let rise. Pat the center down, leave the edges thicker, and turn them up. Brush with egg.

Beat the eggs and sugar lightly, and add cream. Pour the filling into the pie crust. Bake about 25 minutes. The filling should be mildly brown, and still a little shaky. If the filling is too loose, turn the oven off and leave the pie in for 10 minutes. Serve warm or cold.

RASPBERRY-BLUEBERRY TART [VADELMA-MUSTIKKATORTTU]

Crust:
  ½ *cup unbleached white flour*   ¼ *teaspoon sea salt*
  1½ *cups rolled oats*   1 *egg, lightly beaten*
  ¼ *cup sour cream*   ¼ *lb (1 stick) melted butter*

Filling:
  1 *pint raspberries*   2–3 *tablespoons raw sugar*
  ½ *pint blueberries*
  1 *tablespoon potato starch or sweet*
  cookie crumbs

Mix together the flour and rolled oats. Add the sour cream, salt, and lightly beaten egg. Stir in melted butter. Chill to stiffen.

Preheat the oven to 400°F. Grease a 9-inch cake pan. Pat the crust down in it. Bake 15 minutes. Take out and cool a little. Turn the oven to 350°F.

Mix together the raspberries, blueberries, and potato starch or cookie crumbs. Shake until the berries are coated. Spoon the berries into the crust. Sprinkle with sugar. Bake 15 to 20 minutes, or until the berries are juicy and soft. Cool. Cut into wedges and serve.

OATMEAL-APPLE TART [KAURA-OMENATORTTU]

Crust:
3 oz (¾ stick) butter   *½ cup raw sugar*
1½ cups rolled oats   *1 egg, lightly beaten*

Filling:
3–4 tart, juicy apples, peeled, cored,
and sliced

In a heavy frying pan, melt and brown the butter. Add the oats, and let them take on a little color. Add sugar, stir well. Lower the heat, and stir in the lightly beaten egg. Stir, remove from heat.

Preheat the oven to 400°F. Grease well a 9-inch cake pan. Layer the sliced apples on the bottom. Pour the crust mixture over, and pat down. Bake about 20 minutes, or until the top is light brown. Let cool in the pan, and when cold, turn upside down. Cut into wedges and serve.

CHRISTMAS PASTRIES [JOULUTORTUT]

Filling:
½ lb pitted prunes, soaked until   *1 cup water, or more, if needed*
plump   *Juice of ½ lemon*

Crust:
1-2/3 cups unbleached white pastry   *¾ cup heavy cream, whipped*
flour   *¼ lb (1 stick) butter, softened*
½ teaspoon baking powder

Glaze:
1 egg

To make the filling, simmer the soaked prunes in water until very soft and easily mashed. Add more water, if necessary. Mash the prunes while still warm. The mixture should be the consistency of apple sauce. Season with lemon juice. Cool. For the crust, mix together the flour and baking powder. Stir the flour into the whipped cream. Knead in the softened butter. Shape the dough into a ball, and chill until it's hard.

On a floured board, roll out the crust ¼ inch thick. Cut out circles about 4 inches in diameter. Put the circles into the refrigerator until ready to be filled.

Preheat the oven to 450°F. Put about 1 teaspoon of the filling on one half of each pastry circle. Fold the other side over to make a half-moon. Pinch the edges together. Brush the pastries with egg, and bake about 10 minutes, or until brown.

Serve warm with coffee. If you freeze or keep them chilled, reheat them in a rather hot oven, and not wrapped in foil.
Yield: 25 to 30 pastries.

Cakes

It is not easy to tell for sure, which of the cake and cookie recipes are truly or originally Finnish. Cake recipes are the fastest to travel from cook to cook; this was so especially in the old days, when trading cake recipes was a favorite pastime.

These cake recipes are all commonly known in Finland, and have been baked in homes for years, some since the beginning of the century or longer. I have tried to include ones that are not overly sweet, that keep well, and have at least some good nutrients.

SUGAR CAKE [SOKERIKAKKU]

This cake is probably the best known in Finland. Similar to sponge cake, it is light and tasty by itself, or dampened with lemon juice or wine. Often it is decorated with fruits and whipped cream.

Bread crumbs	2 tablespoons cold water
4–5 eggs (1 cup)	¾ cup unbleached white flour
1 cup raw sugar	¼ cup potato starch

Preheat the oven to 350°F. Grease well a 9-inch cake pan, and sprinkle heavily with bread crumbs. Have all this ready.

Beat the eggs and sugar until the mixture is thick and foamy, and pale yellow. Scare the eggs with the cold water. Beat again, until thick.

Mix together the flour and potato starch. Sift it into the eggs, mixing quickly. Do not beat, or whip. Pour into the cake pan, and immediately put it into the oven. Bake 30 to 40 minutes. Do not open the oven during the first 20 minutes. The cake is ready when a knife comes out clean.

Cool the cake, then turn onto a plate. Decorate, or serve plain with coffee.

STRAWBERRY CAKE [MANSIKKAKAKKU]

This is probably the best-known decorated cake, made for birthdays, namedays, weddings, coffee parties. It is fresh and simple, and light.

1 sugar cake (see page 176)	¼ cup water
¼ cup lemon juice	3 tablespoons red berry juice

Filling:
½ cup heavy cream, whipped	1 tablespoon raw sugar
½ pint strawberries, cleaned and mashed	

Frosting:
1 cup heavy cream, whipped
½ teaspoon vanilla extract

1 tablespoon raw sugar (optional)
Whole ripe strawberries

Cut the cake crosswise into two parts, while still warm. Combine the lemon juice, water, and red berry juice, and spoon a little less than half of this mixture over the bottom half of the cake. Top with the top layer, moisten with the rest of the juice.

Whip the cream with vanilla, and sugar, if used, for the frosting. When thick, spoon it over the top and sides of the cake. Decorate with whole strawberries. Chill.

RASPBERRY CAKE [VADELMAKAKKU]

1 sugar cake (see page 176)
1/3 cup pineapple juice

1/3 cup raspberry juice
¼ cup lemon juice

Filling:
1 pint raspberries
2 tablespoons raw sugar

½ cup heavy cream, whipped

Frosting:
1 cup heavy cream, whipped
½ teaspoon vanilla extract
1 tablespoon raw sugar (optional)

½ cup pineapple chunks, fresh or
canned

Slice the cake crosswise into 2 parts. Combine the juices, and spoon a little less than half of the mixture over the bottom layer. Mash the raspberries and sugar, and combine with whipped cream. Spoon the filling over the bottom layer of cake. Cover with the top layer. Spoon the rest of the juice over it.

Whip the cream, vanilla, and sugar, if used, for the frosting. Spoon over the cake, and cover the sides. Decorate with pineapple chunks.

LEMON-CREAM CAKE [SITRUUNA-KERMAKAKKU]

1 sugar cake
¼ cup lemon juice

½ cup orange juice

Filling:
Juice and grated peel of 2 lemons
½ cup raw sugar
1 cup water
3 eggs

1 tablespoon cornstarch or potato
starch
2 tablespoons butter

Frosting:
1 cup heavy cream, whipped
1 tablespoon raw sugar (optional)
¼ teaspoon vanilla extract

Chocolate shavings or
banana slices

Cut the cake crosswise into 2 layers. Combine the juices, and spoon a little less than half on the bottom layer of the cake.

To make the filling, combine the ingredients in a double boiler adding the butter last. Whisk well. Heat, stirring constantly, until the mixture thickens. Let cool, stirring.

Spoon the filling over the bottom layer. Cover with the top layer of the cake. Spoon the rest of the juice over it.

For the frosting whip the cream, vanilla, and sugar, if used, until stiff. Spoon over the top and sides of the cake. Decorate with chocolate shavings or banana slices. Chill.

COFFEE CAKE [KAHVIKAKKU]

This cake with a strong coffee taste is liked by those who don't care for overly sweet things.

Bread crumbs	*¾ cup raisins, soaked until plump*
2 eggs	*¾ cup melted butter or good quality*
2/3 cup raw sugar	*oil*
¾ cup corn syrup or molasses	*¾ cup strong coffee*
(see Note)	*1½ teaspoons baking soda*
1½ teaspoons ground cloves	*¼ cup gluten flour*
1½ teaspoons cinnamon	*2 cups unbleached white flour*

Preheat the oven to 350°F. Grease well a large decorative cake form, or a 2-quart loaf pan, and sprinkle heavily with bread crumbs.

Beat the eggs and sugar well, until foamy and lemon-colored. Add all the other ingredients in the order given. Pour the cake mixture into the form or loaf pan. Bake 1 hour, or until a knife comes out clean.

Let the cake cool before turning it out from the pan. Wrap it in foil, and let stand 1 to 2 days. The taste of the cake improves with a little aging. This cake keeps fresh for a long time.

Note: Use ordinary molasses: blackstrap molasses has a taste that is too strong for the other ingredients.

BUTTERMILK CAKE [PIIMÄKAKKU]

This is one of the quickest, easiest, and tastiest cakes I know of. It's very hard to ruin it, even if you try.

Bread crumbs
¾ cup buttermilk
1 teaspoon baking soda
¼ cup brown sugar
½ cup honey

½ teaspoon ground cloves
½ cup raisins, soaked until plump
½ cup melted butter or good
  quality oil
1-2/3 cups unbleached white flour

Preheat the oven to 350°F. Grease well a cake form or a 2-quart loaf pan, and sprinkle heavily with bread crumbs.

Mix everything together in the order given. Pour the mixture into the pan. Bake 40 to 50 minutes, or until a knife comes out clean. Let cool before turning out of the pan. Wrap in foil. Let "draw" a day or two. Keeps well.

SPICE CAKE [MAUSTEKAKKU]

Bread crumbs
2 eggs
¾ cup raw sugar
1 teaspoon cinnamon
1 teaspoon ginger
2 teaspoons ground orange peel

¼ cup melted butter or good
  quality oil
1 cup sweet or sour cream
1 teaspoon baking soda
1-2/3 cups unbleached white flour

Preheat the oven to 350°F. Grease well a cake form or 2-quart loaf pan, and sprinkle heavily with bread crumbs.

Beat the eggs and sugar until thick. Add cinnamon, ginger, and orange peel. Stir in butter or oil and the cream, into which the soda has been mixed, and then add the flour. Pour into the pan. Bake about 1 hour, or until a knife comes out clean. Cool before turning out of the pan.

CURD CAKE [RAHKAKAKKU]

Bread crumbs
2 eggs
½ cup raw sugar
1 teaspoon ground cardamom
1 teaspoon cinnamon
½ teaspoon ginger
2 teaspoons ground orange peel

1 teaspoon ground lemon peel
1 cup curd, from 1 quart
  buttermilk (see page 188)
½ cup melted butter or good
  quality oil
1½ teaspoons baking powder
1 cup unbleached white flour

Preheat the oven to 400°F. Grease well a 1-quart loaf pan, and sprinkle heavily with bread crumbs.

Beat the eggs and sugar until thick, add the cardamom, cinnamon, ginger, orange peel, and lemon peel. Press the curd through a sieve into the mixture. Stir in the butter or oil, and the flour into which the soda has been mixed. Pour immediately into the pan. Bake 40 to 45 minutes. This cake keeps well.

Cookies

All these cookies are easy and fast to make, and always turn out well. In addition to the ordinary cookies that use white flour, I have found and included a few recipes in which rye, oat, and barley flour are used.

AUNT HANNA'S COOKIES [HANNATÄDIN KAKUT]

One of the easiest and best recipes for cookies you can make even if you've never made cookies before.

¼ lb (1 stick) butter, softened
½ cup raw sugar
1½ cups unbleached white pastry
  flour

½ cup potato starch
2 teaspoons baking powder
½ cup heavy cream

Beat the butter and sugar until white and foamy. Mix together the pastry flour, potato starch, and baking powder. Add a little of the flour mixture to the butter mixture, then add the cream. Quickly stir in the rest of the flour. Do not handle the dough unnecessarily. Chill.

Preheat the oven to 350°F. Grease two cookie sheets. With damp hands, form little round balls from about 1 teaspoon dough for each. Place them well apart on cookie sheets, and flatten a little. Bake 10 to 15 minutes, or until slightly browned. Cool before removing from sheets. Keep in a dry place.

Yield: 35 cookies.

PEASANT COOKIES [TALONPOIKAISLEIVÄT]

¼ lb (1 stick) butter, softened
¼ cup raw sugar
½ teaspoon baking powder
1½ cups unbleached white flour

1 egg
1 tablespoon corn syrup or
  molasses
¼ cup ground almonds

Beat together the butter and sugar. Mix the baking powder into the flour. Beat the egg lightly. Add some flour to the butter mixture, then stir in the molasses, egg, almonds, and the rest of the flour. Make a firm dough, and chill until hard.

Preheat the oven to 400°F. Shape the dough into a long tube, and cut into slices. Put the slices on a greased cookie sheet. Bake about 15 minutes, or until browned a little. Cool before removing from sheet.

Yield: 25 cookies.

CINNAMON COOKIES [KANELIKAKUT]

1 egg
½ cup raw sugar
1 tablespoon cream
1¾ cups unbleached white pastry
   flour

1 teaspoon baking powder
¼ lb (1 stick) butter, softened
1 teaspoon cinnamon

Garnish:
   1 egg
   Sugar

Split almonds

Beat the egg and sugar, add cream and some flour into which the baking powder has been mixed. Stir in the softened butter, cinnamon, and the rest of the flour. Chill.

Preheat the oven to 350°F. On a floured board, roll out the dough about ½ inch thick. Cut small circles. Brush the cakes with egg, sprinkle with sugar, and in the middle of each put a split almond. Bake 10 to 15 minutes.

Yield: 25 cookies.

SMALL COFFEE CAKES [PIENET KAHVILEIVÄT]

Crispy, rich, and dreamy—serve these cookies on your best coffee table.

2 egg yolks
¼ cup raw sugar
2/3 cup unbleached white pastry
   flour
½ cup potato starch

1 teaspoon baking powder
2 tablespoons cream
2 tablespoons melted butter
½ teaspoon vanilla extract

Beat the egg yolks and sugar. Mix together the flour and potato starch. Stir the baking powder into the cream. Add some flour into the egg mixture, add the melted butter, and the cream mixture. Stir in the vanilla and the rest of the flour. Mix quickly. Chill until hard.

Preheat the oven to 350°F. Roll teaspoonsful of the dough into balls and place on a greased cookie sheet. Place the balls somewhat apart. Bake 10 to 15 minutes, or until golden. Cool and remove.

Yield: 20 cookies.

RASPBERRY COOKIES [VADELMALEIVÄT]

3 oz (¾ stick) butter, softened
1 egg
½ cup raw sugar
1 teaspoon baking powder

1¾ cups unbleached white pastry
flour
½ cup sour cream
½ cup raspberry preserves

Beat the softened butter until foamy. Beat the egg and sugar together until thick. Mix the baking powder with the flour. Add a little flour to the egg mixture, then stir in the butter. Add some more flour, and the sour cream. Quickly stir in the rest of the flour. Chill until hard.

Preheat the oven to 350°F. On a floured board, roll the dough out about ½ inch thick. Cut out tiny circles with a cookie cutter. Put the cookies on a greased cookie sheet. Press in the middle of each cake with a finger. Fill the depression with raspberry preserves. Bake the cookies about 15 minutes, or until light brown. Cool on the cookie sheet.
Yield: 25 cookies.

OAT FLOUR COOKIES [KAURAKAKUT]

2 eggs
1/3 cup raw sugar
1½ teaspoons baking powder

2 cups oat flour
¼ lb (1 stick) melted butter
Almond extract

Beat the eggs and sugar well, until thick. Mix the baking powder into the oat flour. Stir some flour into the eggs, add melted butter, a couple of drops of almond extract, and the rest of the flour. Mix quickly. Chill until hard.

Preheat the oven to 400°F. Take a teaspoonful of the dough at a time, and roll it into a small round ball. Put the balls on a greased cookie sheet, well apart. Bake 10 to 15 minutes, or until golden. Cool on the sheet. Store in a dry place.
Yield: 25 cookies.

OATMEAL LACE BREADS [KAURALASTUT]

¼ lb (1 stick) butter
¼ cup raw sugar
1¼ cups rolled oats
2 tablespoons unbleached white
flour

1 tablespoon heavy cream
1 teaspoon ground orange peel
(optional)

Melt the butter in a saucepan, add the sugar, rolled oats, flour, and cream. Stir, bring to a boil, and simmer about 3 minutes. Let cool. Add the orange peel, if used.

Preheat the oven to 350°F. Grease two cookie sheets. Drop 1 teaspoon of dough at a time on the sheet, press down. Let the drops stand well apart, for they will spread while baking. Bake about 10 minutes, or until the cookies are spread out and browned. Cool before removing.
Yield: 25 cookies.

GRANDMA'S BARLEY COOKIES [MUMMON OHRAKAKUT]

No one will ever guess that these cookies are made of barley. They are spicy with a nice coarse texture.

1 egg	½ cup cream
¼ cup raw sugar	1 teaspoon baking powder
1-2/3 cups barley flour	½ teaspoon ginger
1/3 cup melted butter	1 teaspoon cinnamon
1/3 cup corn syrup or honey	1 teaspoon ground cardamom

Start the night before. Beat the egg and sugar until thick. Add some barley flour. Stir in the melted butter, corn syrup or honey, and the cream into which the baking powder has been mixed. Stir in the ginger, cinnamon, cardamom, and the rest of the barley flour. Mix well. Let stand in the refrigerator overnight.

Next day, preheat the oven to 400°F. With wet hands, roll each teaspoonful of dough into a ball, put on a greased cookie sheet. Press the cookies with a fork, so there will be tine marks on the surface. Bake about 15 minutes. Cool and remove. Keep in a dry place.

Yield: 30 cookies.

RYE COOKIES [RUISKEKSIT]

Rye cookies are great for making small sandwiches. Try them spread with cream cheese and decorated with a slice of apple.

¼ lb (1 stick) melted butter	1½ teaspoons baking powder
½ cup raw sugar	½ teaspoon sea salt
1 cup unbleached white flour	3–4 tablespoons cold water
1 cup rye flour	

In the order given, mix everything together into a firm dough. Shape into a ball, and chill until hard.

Preheat the oven to 350°F. On a floured board, roll the dough out about ½ inch thick. With a cookie form, cut out small circles, and put them on greased cookie sheets. Bake about 15 minutes. Cool before removing. Keep in a dry place.

Yield: 25 cookies.

Chapter 12

MILK, CHEESE, AND EGGS
[MAITO–, JUUSTO– JA MUNARUUAT]

Milk and buttermilk are in Finland the main table drinks with meals, although lately light beer has won much popularity. The consumption of milk and milk products is considerable in Finland. These few recipes give an example of milk products that can still be made at home with very little trouble. They are very satisfying to make, as one can clearly see the changes taking place when one product turns into another.

FINNISH YOGURT [VIILI]

Viili is a yogurt-like sour milk product, sold in Finland commercially and also made at home. It is produced by the same type of bacteria that make yogurt, but it is milder in taste, somehow nutty, and creamier in quality.

There are two kinds of *viili*: long and short. The long *viili* is called so because it stretches. It is the more popular one and also tastier. For making it, you do need a *viili* starter to produce the right kind of bacteria. The short *viili* doesn't have the elastic quality, and is not as smooth in taste. I have made short *viili* by using buttermilk as a starter. Some Finns who live in the United States may have the *viili* starter—if you know one, ask for some. The best *viili* is made from country-fresh whole milk.

1 teaspoon buttermilk or starter   *1½ cups milk, regular or nonfat*

Use a very clean dessert bowl. Put the starter or buttermilk at the bottom of the bowl. Heat the milk to lukewarm, and pour over the buttermilk. Stir a little to mix the starter.

Let the *viili* stand at room temperature 1 day. The bacteria will thicken it. Be sure not to shake the *viili* while it's forming, otherwise it will become watery. During a thunderstorm the *viili* is often ruined because it separates. The place where you make the *viili* must be dark and draftless. Shelves of a closet are a good place.

When the *viili* has thickened, chill it.

Take a few spoons of the last bowl of *viili* you eat, and use it for making a new batch. You may keep the starter in a cold place a few days, but not too long. When you take the starter, include some of the white mold from the top of the *viili* bowl. This is the most delicious part, and this way your *viili* will have more vitamin B in it.

It is best when served cold. In Finland, especially in the countryside, *viili* is often eaten with a flour called *talkkuna,* which is made differently in different parts of Finland, but usually is a mixture of oats, barley, and ground dried peas. The grains are sweetened, and sometimes smoked lightly, then dried. *Viili* is also served with sugar and cinnamon or ginger sprinkled on top, or with berries and sugar. Some people like it plain, or just with some sugar.

Servings: 1.

HOMEMADE CURD [RAHKA]

The curd, or milk solids, is actually a kind of cheese, close to farmer's or cottage cheese, and can be eaten in the same way. But in Finland, especially in the old Karelian cooking, curd is used in many recipes as an ingredient. The easiest way to make curd is from buttermilk.

2 quarts buttermilk

Preheat the oven to 200°F. Pour the buttermilk into a large kettle or oven casserole. Leave it in the oven for 2 to 3 hours. During this time the curd will separate from the liquid, the whey. Curd will rise to the surface. Do not ever let the buttermilk boil. The longer you bake it, the harder and more solid the curd will get.

Line a sieve with two or three thicknesses of cheesecloth. With a slotted spoon, peel the curd off and put through the sieve into a bowl. Press down to squeeze out all liquid. Pick up the edges of cheesecloth, and tie together. Put a weight on the curd, and let stand overnight.

Reserve the whey. For most recipes in this book, the curd will have to be ground or pressed through a sieve. Good curd is very dry, and has a pleasantly sour taste. Use the mildly sour whey as a tasty base for other dishes. Whey still has vitamins and minerals in it. Use it as the liquid base for breads that call for water. It gives an interesting additional taste to yeast breads. Use it as a base for cereal soups and porridges, when the recipe calls for water. Or use it as the base for other soups, if the tastes of the other ingredients agree with it. Try it out!

Yield: 2 cups.

FRUIT CURD [HEDELMÄRAHKA]

Use your imagination for fruit combinations.

1 cup curd　　　　　　　　　　　*Honey to taste*
1/3 cup heavy cream, whipped　　*Fresh berries or fruits*

Grind the curd fine. Blend with whipped cream, honey, and berries. Chill and serve from dessert bowls.

With the curd you can add crushed pineapple, orange juice and orange peel with a little vanilla, fresh or frozen raspberries, raspberries with chopped peaches and vanilla, mashed strawberries, or orange juice with chopped peaches and vanilla.

Servings: 2.

CURD MAYONNAISE [RAHKAMAJONEESI]

1 egg　　　　　　　　　　　　　　*¼ teaspoon paprika (optional)*
2 tablespoons lemon juice　　　　*1 cup finely ground curd*
½ teaspoon sea salt　　　　　　　*1 cup vegetable oil*
1 teaspoon prepared mustard

Beat the egg, add the lemon juice, salt, and mustard. Add paprika, if used. Blend in the curd, which must be finely ground or pressed through a sieve. Rub well with a wooden spoon.

Drop the oil in, little by little, beating well after each addition. First add just a couple of drops, then increase the amount of oil. Keep in a cold place.

Serve on salads, as you would mayonnaise. Very good on smoked fish, ham, and potato salads.

Yield: 1 pint.

EGG CHEESE [MUNAJUUSTO]

Also called Easter cheese, it is a mild and beautifully delicate cheese to have either for lunch or to serve on a dessert tray.

2 quarts milk	*3 cups buttermilk*
Cream (optional for a richer cheese)	*1½ teaspoons sea salt*
4 eggs	*1 teaspoon raw sugar*

Pour the milk, or a mixture of milk and cream, into a large kettle. Heat, and bring to a boil. Beat the eggs, and add the buttermilk; beat until mixed well. Remove the hot milk from heat. Slowly pour the egg-buttermilk mixture into it, beating all the time.

Bring the mixture to a boil. Now you should see the solids starting to separate as the milk curdles. Just when the milk starts to boil again, lift away from the heat. Add salt and sugar. Stir well. Put it into a warm place (200°F. oven) and let stand until the solids rise to the surface.

Use either a wooden cheese mold or a sieve for molding the cheese. Put a damp cheesecloth into the mold or sieve, and with a slotted spoon, remove the solid from the whey, into the mold. Press down, and tie the cheesecloth around the cheese.

Put the cheese in a cold place, let stand overnight. Turn it out from the mold. It may be eaten as it is but is even better when baked. Bake it at 450°F for 10 to 15 minutes, or until the top has nicely browned.

Serve for lunch with bread, on a smorgasbord, or to end a meal. Eat it when it's fresh; it won't keep more than a few days.

Yield: 2 lbs cheese.

EGG CASSEROLE [MUNALAATIKKO]

4 eggs	*8 strips bacon, browned and cubed*
2 cups light cream	*Salt to taste (optional)*

Preheat the oven to 350°F. Beat the eggs and light cream together. Add the bacon cubes and salt, if used. Grease well an oven casserole or a 1-quart loaf pan, and pour the mixture in.

Bake 15 to 20 minutes, or until just set, but still a little shaky. The custardy structure makes it different from regular omelets.

Serve hot as a lunch or breakfast main dish. It is also served as a side dish with fish or meat. Serve cold leftovers on a sandwich.

Servings: 2 to 4.

JAM OMELET [HILLOMUNAKAS]

6 eggs   *Confectioners' sugar*
2 cups cream
1 cup jam, strawberry, raspberry or
  other

Beat the eggs, add cream. Preheat the oven to 350°F. Grease a 9-inch cake or pie pan. Pour the mixture in it. Bake 20 to 30 minutes, or until the omelet has set, but is still a little shaky, and not dry. The surface must be light brown.

Spread the jam on a large round plate. Turn the omelet on top of the jam. Dust it with confectioners' sugar.

Serve warm or cold for dessert. I sometimes serve it as a breakfast treat.
Servings: 4 to 6.

Chapter 13

BEVERAGES
[JUOMAT]

Before the growth of the soda industry, the soft drinks and juices were made at home. In Finland, steamed berry juice concentrates are still very much loved; in the winter black currant juice is drunk steaming hot as a remedy for colds—or just cold feet.

The most popular homemade drink is the May Day *sima,* a simple-to-make lemon drink, a children's favorite. I have used recipes that use honey instead of sugar, and are also inexpensive to make. If the children learn to like the taste, they are good to have as an occasional sweet drink instead of the sugared, carbonated sodas.

OLD-FASHIONED COFFEE [KAHVI]

As soon as coffee was introduced to Finland, it became a very popular drink. The Finns are still among the top coffee drinkers in the world.

Water
1–2 *heaping teaspoons of coarsely*
    ground coffee per cup of water

Fill the clean coffee pot with as much water as you need. Measure the coffee and pour into the pot. Bring to a boil. There will be foam formed on top of the pot. You should never let the coffee boil. Just when it reaches the boiling point and starts to bubble, remove the pot from heat.

Scare the coffee by pouring in about ¼ cup ice water. Put the lid on, and let stand about 5 minutes. The coffee will settle to the bottom. Sometimes coffee clearer is added to the pot after it has been removed from the heat (see below).

Be sure not to shake the coffee pot, when you pour into cups. The coffee pot is usually left on the table, covered with a padded coffee hat, *kahvipannunmyssy*, to keep it warm.

Spring water is the best water for making coffee.

COFFEE CLEARER [KAHVINSELVIKE]

In the old days, coffee clearer was used to help the coffee clear up better and sooner. It was made of large fish scales, usually of the scales of bream.

The scales are rinsed thoroughly under running water. Then they are soaked in salted water for some time. They are then drained, and spread on a towel to dry. Finally, they are dried on paper.

A couple of scales were dropped into a pot of coffee as a clearer.

MAY DAY DRINK [SIMA]

There are as many *sima* recipes as there are cooks. This is a nice recipe, because it uses honey.

2 lemons	2 cups light beer
5 quarts water	¼ teaspoon ground ginger (optional)
2 cups light honey	4–5 raisins per bottle
1 teaspoon active dry yeast	

Peel the lemon thinly, making sure you don't take any of the white part. Peel off and discard the white. Slice the lemon very thin. Put the lemon slices and peels with the water and honey into a large kettle. Bring to a boil, cover, and simmer about 15 minutes. Remove from heat, and let cool, still covered, until lukewarm.

Add the yeast, beer, and ginger, if used. Let stand at room temperature about 12 hours. Drain, and pour the drink into sterile bottles. Add 4 to 5 raisins per bottle. Cap tightly and let stand 1 week in a cold place.

HONEY DRINK [HUNAJAJUOMA]

4 quarts water	2 lemons, sliced thin
1½ cups honey	½ teaspoon active dry yeast

Heat the water, and dissolve the honey in it. Add the lemon slices, cover the kettle and simmer about 1 hour.

Let the mixture cool until it's merely warm. Dissolve the yeast in it, mix well. Cover, and let stand at room temperature about 12 hours.

Pour the drink through a sieve into clean, sterilized bottles. Cap tightly. Keep in a cold place for 5 or 6 days before serving. Refrigerated, the drink will keep a couple of weeks.

CHRISTMAS GLÖGG [JOULUGLÖGI]

The drinking of *glögg* starts at the First Sunday of Advent, and can be continued with good conscience until the New Year. In Finland people—in offices as well as at home—use every excuse to have *glögg* parties. If the spirit rises high and refuses to land, the parties continue until the small hours.

  1 *bottle cheap red wine*
2–3 *tablespoons Madeira*
  ½ *cup raw sugar, or to taste*
1/3 *cup raisins*
1–2 *sticks cinnamon*
5–6 *whole cloves*
  ¼ *cup blanched, slivered almonds*
  ¼ *cup vodka to spike it up*
    (*optional*)

In a large kettle, combine all the ingredients except the vodka. Heat slowly, until the drink is steaming hot. Stir every now and then, and taste with a spoon whenever you feel like it. Do not let the drink get even close to boiling. Just keep it warm. Before serving, add vodka if you wish.

    Servings: 1 to 6.

ICE COLD SCHNAPPS [SNAPSI]

Cold schnapps is a ritualistic drink, served with the smorgasbord, often with raw fish dishes—and, of course, with crayfish. In Finland the national *Koskenkorva,* known in America as Finlandia Vodka—is the favorite.

Chill the bottle of vodka in the freezer a couple of hours. The bottle should be frosty outside, when it's served. If you want to be fancy, chill the tiny schnapps glasses also until they frost.

Just before serving, pour out the schnapps. Keep the bottle in ice. With schnapps, mineral water or beer is served from goblets. The truly chilled schnapps has a clear non-taste—it should feel almost like vapors in your throat. But you will feel instantly how it warms your stomach.

There are many rituals, and it's fun to follow at least a couple of them. Some people take their schnapps drinking very seriously: the more schnapps they have had, the more serious they get. Usually the first sip of schnapps is drunk together. The host raises his glass, and all the others follow. This is often followed by a lot of nodding around. The nodding means "To your health," which is actually said sometimes.

There are other things one can say. The originally Swedish *Skål!* is widely used in Finland, but it's rather formal and proper. The Finnish word is *Kippis!* and some people think it a little vulgar; therefore, it's used for fun. New words are introduced wherever there are friends drinking schnapps, in the same manner as a loved child is given many nicknames. Surprise your Finnish friends by saying *Hölkynkölkyn* in the Savo accent, if someone will teach you how. It's a nonsense word, and sounds fun!

Some people insist the whole glass of schnapps should be had all at once. If someone says *Pohjanmaan kautta*, that's what they mean. The sentence doesn't mean anything of the kind, but there is another phrase that sounds similar and means "To the bottom," so of course we use the one that doesn't mean it. If you consider schnapps drinking a sport, you will follow suit.

RHUBARB DRINK [RAPARPERIJUOMA]

2 lbs raw sugar or honey　　　　　　　*2 lbs rhubarb, cut into cubes*
5 quarts water, preferably spring　　*1 teaspoon active dry yeast*
　water

Dissolve the sugar or honey in the water, add the rhubarb cubes, and bring to a quick rolling boil. Let boil for about 2 minutes. Cool.

When the drink is merely warm, dissolve the yeast in it. Stir well. Let stand at room temperature about 12 hours.

Drain the drink, and discard the rhubarb pulp. Pour the drink into sterile bottles. Cap tightly. Keep in a cool place 4 to 5 days before serving.

　Serve chilled.

Index